AMERICAN WOMEN
images and realities

AMERICAN WOMEN
Images and Realities

Advisory Editors
ANNETTE K. BAXTER
LEON STEIN

A Note About This Volume

In this powerful survey of the status of woman midway through the Twenties, Suzanne La Follette raised fundamental, disturbing questions about the battle for equality and the vote. That battle had been fought within a world shaped by men, with values they held dear, with goals they had set. It was a world of injustice and oppression, making a mockery out of equality. This book is an eloquent plea for consideration of the larger issues to which the status and progress of women are linked: war, the nature of work and economic justice.

CONCERNING WOMEN

by
SUZANNE LA FOLLETTE

ARNO PRESS
A New York Times Company
New York • 1972

301.412
L165c

Reprint Edition 1972 by Arno Press Inc.

Reprinted from a copy in The Wesleyan
University Library

American Women: Images and Realities
ISBN for complete set: 0-405-04445-3
See last pages of this volume for titles.

Manufactured in the United States of America

- - - - - - - - - - - - -

Library of Congress Cataloging in Publication Data

La Follette, Suzanne.
 Concerning women.

 (American women: images and realities)
 Reprint of the 1926 ed.
 1. Woman--Social and moral questions. 2. Marriage.
I. Title. II. Series.
HQ1206.L3 1972   301.41'2   72-2610
ISBN 0-405-04464-X

CONCERNING WOMEN

CONCERNING WOMEN

by
SUZANNE LA FOLLETTE

ALBERT & CHARLES BONI
NEW YORK   1926

Copyright, 1926, by Albert & Charles Boni, Inc.

Manufactured in the United States of America

To
ELLEN WINSOR
and
REBECCA WINSOR EVANS

CONTENTS

CHAPTER		PAGE
I	The Beginnings of Emancipation	1
II	Woman's Status, Past and Present	19
III	Institutional Marriage and Its Economic Aspects	56
IV	Woman and Marriage	93
V	The Economic Position of Women	157
VI	What is to be Done	207
VII	Signs of Promise	270

Let there be, then, no coercion established in society, and the common law of gravity prevailing, the sexes will fall into their proper places.

MARY WOLLSTONECRAFT.

CHAPTER I

THE BEGINNINGS OF EMANCIPATION

It will be foolish to assume that women are free, until books about them shall have ceased to have more than an antiquarian interest. All such books, including this one, imply by their existence that women may be regarded as a class in society; that they have in common certain characteristics, conditions or disabilities which, predominating over their individual variations, warrant grouping them on the basis of sex. No such assumption about men would be thinkable. Certain masculine qualities, so-called, may be singled out by amateur psychologists and opposed to certain feminine qualities, so-called; but from books about the sphere of man, the rights of man, the intelligence of man, the psychology of man, the soul of man, our shelves are mercifully free. Such books may one day appear, but when they do it will mean that society has passed from its present state through a state of sex-equality and into a state of female domination. In that day, in place of the edifying spectacle of men proclaiming that woman is useful only as a bearer of children, society may behold the equally edifying spectacle of women proclaiming that man is useful only as a begetter of children; since it seems to be characteristic of the dominant sex to regard the other sex chiefly as a source of pleasure and as a means of reproduction. It seems also to be characteristic of the dominant sex—I judge from the world's experience during the domination of men— to regard itself as humanity, and the other sex as a class of somewhat lower beings created by Providence for its convenience and enjoyment; just as it is characteristic of a dominant class, such as an aristocracy, to regard the lower classes as being created solely for the purpose of supporting its power and doing its will. When once a social order is well established, no matter what injustice it involves, those who occupy a position of advantage are not long in coming to believe that it is the only possible and reasonable order, and imposing their belief, by force if necessary, on those whom circumstances have placed in their power. There is nothing more innately human than the tendency to

The Beginnings of Emancipation 3

transmute what has become customary into what has been divinely ordained.

Thus among the Hebrews the subordination of woman gave rise to the notion that she was fashioned out of man's rib. She was the result of a divine afterthought, the *sexus sequior* of the ancients and more recently of Schopenhauer, "inferior in every respect to the first." Since the Divine Artist had had good practice in creating Adam, it might logically have been expected that His second sex would turn out even better than His first; we must therefore lay His failure to the somewhat sketchy nature of the materials He chose to work with. This Hebrew myth of the creation of woman has had considerable effect on her status in the era known as Christian. Being "only a supernumerary bone," as Bossuet reminded her, she could naturally not aspire to a position of equality with man. She must remember her origin, and be humble and subservient as befitted a mere rib.

She was humble and subservient, as a matter of fact, for an incredibly long time; so long that there exists a general suspicion even at the present day that there is something in her nature which makes her want to be subject to man and to live as it were at second hand. This thought would be even more alarming than it is, perhaps, if it were not true that men themselves have stood for a good deal of subjection during the world's known history. Chattel slavery and serfdom were abolished from the civilized world only at about the time that the subjection of women began to be modified; and men still endure, not only with resignation but with positive cheerfulness, a high degree of industrial and political slavery. The man who is entirely dependent for his livelihood upon the will of an employer is an industrial slave, and the man who may be drafted into an army and made to fight and perhaps die for a cause in which he can have no possible interest is the slave of the State; yet one can not see that this proves Aristotle's assumption that there are free natures and slave natures, any more than the subjection of women proves that they want to be subjected. What the slavery of men, as of women, implies is the existence of an economic and social order that is inimical to their interests as human beings; and it implies nothing more than this.

Nor does the opposition to the emancipation of women which still finds expression in this country and in Europe, prove anything more than that superstitious addiction to custom of which I have already spoken. Those anxious critics who protest that women have got more freedom than is good for Society make the mistake of supposing that Society can exist only if its organization remains unchanged. The same conservatism has opposed all the revolutionary adaptations which have fitted the social order to the breakdown of old forms and their replacement by new ones. Yet when the need for such adaptations ceases, the growth of the social organism ceases with it, and we have such a spectacle of arrested development as the civilization of India presents. Society, in so far as it has become organic, is governed by the same rules as any other organism: the condition of its health is growth, and growth is change.

Certainly the present tendency of woman to assume a position of equality with man involves, and will continue even more to involve, profound psychic and material readjustments. But to assume that such readjustments will injure or destroy Society is to adopt toward Society an attitude of philosophical realism, to attribute to it a personality, to suppose that it is equally capable of destruction with the individual, and that it may in some mystical way derive benefit from the sacrifice of the individual's best interests. But what is Society save an aggregation of individuals, half male, half female? Where you have a handful of people forming a community, there you have Society; and if the individuals are enlightened and humane it may be called a civilized Society, if they are ignorant and brutal it will be uncivilized. To assume that its "interests" may be promoted by the enslavement of one-half its members, is unreasonable. One may be permitted the doubtful assumption that this enslavement promotes the welfare of the other half of Society, but it is obvious that it can not promote the welfare of the whole, unless we assume that slavery is beneficial to the slave (the classic assumption, indeed, where the slaves have been women). When we consider the political organization known as the State, we have a different matter. The State always represents the organized interest of a dominant class; therefore the subjection of other classes may be said to benefit the State, and their emancipation may be opposed as a danger to the State.

It is evident from the very nature of the State [1]

---

[1] For a most enlightening treatment of the genesis and nature of the State, I refer my readers to Franz Oppenheimer's short treatise on the subject ("The State," B. W. Huebsch, Inc., New York). It is

The Beginnings of Emancipation 7

that its interests are opposed to those of Society; and while the complete emancipation of women, as I shall show later, would undoubtedly imply the destruction of the State, since it must accrue from the emancipation of other subject classes, their emancipation, far from destroying Society, must be of inestimable benefit to it. Those critics, and there are many, who argue that women must submit to restrictions upon their freedom for the good of the State, as well as those advocates of woman's rights who argue that women must be emancipated for the good of the State, simply fail to make this vital distinction between the State and Society; and their failure to do so is one of the potent reasons why the nonsense that has been written about women is limited only by the literature of the subject.

Feminist and anti-feminist arguments from this

sufficient here to define it as an organization primarily designed to perpetuate the division of Society into an owning and exploiting class and a landless, exploited class. In its genesis it is an organization of a conquering group, by means of which that group maintains its economic exploitation of those subjugated. In its later stages, when the conquering class has become merely an owning class, the State is an organization controlled by this class through its control of wealth, for the purpose of protecting ownership against the propertyless classes and facilitating their exploitation by the owning class. The State is thus the natural enemy of all its citizens except those of the owning class.

standpoint centre in the function of childbearing; therefore it should be noted that the emphasis which is placed on this function by the interest of the State is quite different from the emphasis that would be placed upon it by the interest of Society; for the interest of the State is numerical, while the interest of Society is qualitative. The State requires as many subjects as possible, both as labour-motors and as fighters. The interest of Society, on the other hand, is the interest of civilization: if a community is to be wholesome and intelligent, it is necessary not that the individuals who compose it shall be as numerous as possible, but that they shall be as wholesome and intelligent as possible. In general, the interest of the State is promoted by the number of its subjects; that of Society by the quality of its members.

The interest of the State in this respect has been most concisely expressed by Nietzsche. "Man," said he, "shall be trained for war, and woman for the re-creation of the warrior: all else is folly"; and if one accept his premises he is exactly right. But there have been many writers on women who have not accepted his premises—not at least without qualification—and who have yet failed to ob-

The Beginnings of Emancipation

serve the antithesis between the interest which the State has, and the interest which Society has, in the question of population. Hence, mingled with the voices of those critics who have demanded the subjection of woman for the sake of children, have been the voices of other critics demanding her emancipation for the sake of children: and both these schools of critics have overlooked her claim to freedom on her own behalf. It is for the sake of humanity, and not for the sake of children, that women ought to have equal status with men. That children will gain enormously by the change is true; but this is beside the issue, which is justice.

The argument that woman must be free for the sake of the race, is an argument of expediency; as nine-tenths of the arguments against her legal subjection have been, and indeed had to be. Unfortunately, humanity is likely to turn a deaf ear to the claims of justice, especially when they conflict with established abuses, unless these claims are backed by the claims of expediency plus a good measure of necessity. Adventitious circumstances have made the social recognition of woman's claims a necessity, and their political recognition a matter of expediency. Otherwise she would have to wait much longer for the establishment of her rights as man's equal than now appears likely. In the Western world her battle is very largely won; full equality, social, industrial and legal, seems to be only a matter of time and tactics. This she owes to the great political and industrial revolutions of the eighteenth century.

The conscious movement towards freedom for women may be said to have originated in the great emancipatory movement which found expression in the American and French revolutions. The revolutionists did not succeed in establishing human freedom; they poured the new wine of belief in equal rights for all men into the old bottle of privilege for some; and it soured. But they did succeed in creating political forms which admitted, in theory at least, the principle of equality. Their chief contribution to progress was that they dramatically and powerfully impressed the idea of liberty upon the minds of men, and thus altered the whole course of human thought. Mary Wollstonecraft's book, "A Vindication of the Rights of Women," revolutionary though it seemed in its day, was a perfectly natural and logical application of this idea of liberty to the situation of her sex. This remarkable book may be said

The Beginnings of Emancipation

to have marked the beginning of the conscious movement towards the emancipation of women.

The unconscious movement was the outgrowth of the revolution in industry, brought about by the introduction of the machine. Women had always been industrial workers, but their work, after the break-up of the gilds, was for the most part carried on at home. When the factory supplanted the family as the producing unit in society, the environment of women was altered; and the change affected not only those women who followed industry to the factories, but also those who remained housewives, for where these had before been required to perform, or at least to superintend, a large amount of productive work, they now found their function, as the family became a consuming unit, reduced to the superintendence of expenditures and the operation of the household machinery—a labour which was increasingly lightened by the progress of invention. With domestic conditions so changed, what was more natural than that the daughters should go into the factory; or, if the family were well-to-do, into the schools, which were forced reluctantly to open their doors to women? And what was more natural than that women, as their minds were developed through education, should perceive the injustice and humiliation of their position, and organize to defend their right to recognition as human beings? "If we dared," says Stendhal, "we would give girls the education of a slave. . . . Arm a man and then continue to oppress him, and you will see that he can be so perverse as to turn his arms against you as soon as he can."

Women in the factories and shops; women in the schools—from this it was only a moment to their invasion of the professions, and not a very long time until they would be invading every field that had been held the special province of men. This is the great unconscious and unorganized woman's movement which has aroused such fear and resentment among people who saw it without understanding it.

The organized movement may be regarded simply as an attempt to get this changing relation of women to their environment translated into the kind of law that the eighteenth century had taught the world to regard as just: law based on the theory of equal rights for all human beings. The opposition that the movement encountered offers ample testimony to the fact that "acceptance in principle" is more than a mere subterfuge of diplomats and politicians.

The Beginnings of Emancipation 13

The eighteenth and nineteenth centuries resolutely clung to the theory of equality, and as resolutely opposed its logical application. This is not surprising; most people, no doubt, when they espouse human rights, make their own mental reservations about the proper application of the word "human." Women had hardly been regarded as human in mediaeval Europe; they were considered something a little more from the chivalrous point of view, and something a little less from the more common, workaday standpoint. The shadow of this old superstition still clouded the minds of men: therefore it is hardly surprising that the egalitarians of the French Revolution excluded women from equal political and legal rights with men; and that the young American republic which had adopted the Declaration of Independence, continued to sanction the slavery of negroes and the subjection of women. How firmly rooted this superstition was, may be seen in the following irresistibly funny excerpt from the writings of that great American advocate of freedom, the author of the Declaration, Thomas Jefferson.

Were our State a pure democracy, in which all its

inhabitants should meet together to transact all their business, there would yet be excluded from their deliberations (1) infants until arrived at years of discretion. (2) Women, who, to prevent depravation of morals and ambiguity of issue, could not mix promiscuously in the public meetings of men. (3) Slaves.

Thus does superstition cast out logic. Nor does superstition die easily. The masculine assumption, usually quite unconscious, that women are unfit for freedom, bids fair to persevere as stubbornly as the feminine assumption that marriage offers a legitimate and established mode of extortion.[1]

If the conscious feminists bore the brunt of the resentment aroused by woman's changing relation to the world about her, it was because their opponents did them the honour of believing that they were responsible for the change. It was a strangely

---

[1] I shall take up this question later; but I might remark that this point is well illustrated by a suit recently brought in the State of New York. The former wife of a wealthy man, whom he had divorced twenty years before, brought action against him for separation and maintenance. When asked why she had waited twenty years before questioning the validity of the divorce and her husband's subsequent remarriage, her lawyer stated that *she had never been in need of money before*, but that she had been swindled out of the money settled upon her by her husband at the time of the divorce. The italics are mine; and no comment, I think, is needed.

incurious attitude that permitted such an assumption to be held; for it really takes a very feeble exercise of intelligence to perceive that a handful of feminist agitators could hardly coax millions of women into industry—under conditions often extremely disadvantageous—into business, the schools and the professions. I believe the cause of this incuriousness lay in the very fear aroused by these changes and the social revaluations which they implied; fear for a relation between the sexes which, having been established for so long, seemed the only reasonable, or indeed possible, relation. Filled as they were with this fear of change, which is one of the strongest human emotions, the opponents of woman's emancipation were incapable of objectivity. Their intellectual curiosity was paralyzed. This accounts, perhaps, for the utterances of two such eminent philosophers as Schopenhauer and Nietzsche. They came to the subject strongly prejudiced: the idea of any claims on behalf of women filled them with disgust; therefore, as one may take a certain malicious pleasure in observing, their thought on the subject was hampered by that "weakness of the reasoning faculty" which Schopenhauer found characteristic of women. If, when discussing woman, they had not been as "childish, frivolous and short-sighted" as they believed women to be, they might, along with lesser minds, have arrived at some understanding of a subject which has always been thought much more mysterious and baffling than it really is. The woman of their day may have been the poor creature they pronounced her to be, but if she was, the obvious question was, Why? Was she a poor creature by nature, or because of centuries of adaptation to a certain kind of life? This question neither Schopenhauer nor Nietzsche took the trouble to ask. They weighed her as she was—or as they thought she was—and arrived at the sage conclusion that the West had much to learn from the Orient concerning the proper attitude toward her.

It would be a very desirable thing [says Schopenhauer] if this Number Two of the human race were in Europe also relegated to their natural place [which he conceives to be the harem of a polygamous household] and an end put to this lady-nuisance, which not only moves all Asia to laughter but would have been ridiculed by Greece and Rome as well.

Nietzsche, in the same vein, remarks that

The Beginnings of Emancipation

a man who has depth of spirit as well as of desires, and has also the depth of benevolence which is capable of severity and harshness, and easily confounded with them, can only think of woman as Orientals do: he must conceive of her as a possession, as confinable property, as a being predestined for service and accomplishing her mission therein.

Such a view of the "weaker sex" of course proves nothing about women, but it proves a good deal about the effect that their subjection has had on the minds of men. It is a significant fact that both Schopenhauer and Nietzsche were Germans, and that in their day the status of women was lower in Germany than in any other important country of the Western World, except Italy.

The corruption of both sexes that results from the subjection of one, has been too convincingly dealt with by other writers to need discussion here. What I should like to emphasize is the futility of approaching the so-called "woman question" with any sort of pre-conceived notion concerning the nature of woman, or her sphere, or her duty to the State or to Society; and above all, of approaching it with the idea—the idea that obsesses all reformers—that she is a more or less passive creature about whom something either ought or ought not to be done, or, for that matter, about whom something can be done. What she should and can do for herself is a different matter; and to that question I intend to address myself before I leave this subject.

CHAPTER II

WOMAN'S STATUS, PAST AND PRESENT

I

WOMAN tends to assume a position of equality with man only where the idea of property in human beings has not yet arisen or where it has disappeared: that is to say, only in extremely primitive or highly civilized communities. In all the intermediate stages of civilization, woman is in some degree regarded as a purchasable commodity. Her status varies widely among different peoples: there are primitive tribes where she holds a position of comparative independence; and there are civilized peoples, on the other hand, among whom she is virtually a slave. But always there is present the idea of subordination to a male owner, husband, father or brother, even though it may survive only in ceremonial observances, *e. g.*, in the ritual practice of "giving in marriage," or in certain legal disabilities, such, for instance, as the law entitling a man to his wife's services without remuneration.

The subjection of women, then, bears a close intrinsic resemblance to both chattel slavery and industrial slavery, in that its basis is economic. As soon as civilization advances to the point of a rudimentary organization of agriculture and industry, woman becomes valuable as a labour-motor and a potential producer of children who will become labour-motors and fighters. Her economic value, or chattel-value, then, is a commodity for which her family may demand payment; and hence, apparently, arises the custom of exacting a bride-price from the man who wishes to marry her. Once established, this custom of barter in marriage strikes root so deeply that the woman who has brought no bride-price is often regarded with scorn and her children considered illegitimate; and the idea of male ownership that accompanies it becomes so pronounced that it persists even where, owing to an excess of women coupled with monogamy, the custom has been practically reversed, and the father buys a husband for his daughter. An instance of this survival is the system of dowry which exists in France. Unless it is otherwise stipulated by pre-nuptial agreement, the dowry is at the disposal of the husband, and the wife, under the law, owes him obedience.

When the bargain has been made and the bride delivered to her husband's family, her services generally become, save in tribes where residence is matrilocal, the property of her purchasers, and she is subject to her husband, or, where the patriarchal system is highly developed, to the head of his tribe. It must be remarked, however, that although this is the usual arrangement, it is not invariable. Among some peoples, the husband's rights are purely sexual, the services of the wife, and often even her children, belonging to her own tribe; and among others, the husband must pay for his bride in services which render him for a long period the virtual slave of his wife's relatives. The point to be remarked in all this is that any conception of woman as an individual entity, as in any sense belonging to herself, and not to her own relatives or to her husband and his family, seems to be practically non-existent among primitive peoples, as it was until recently among civilized peoples. But it must be remarked, too, that in this respect her position is only less desirable than that of the man; for in primitive society the group so dominates the individual that in almost every phase of life he is hedged about with restrictions and taboos which leave little room for the play of personality and the pursuit of individual desires. All social advancement has been in the direction of the individual's escape from this group-tyranny.

So important is the part that the labour of women plays in the primitive world, that the wife or wives are often the sole support of husband and family; and a man's wealth and social prestige may actually depend upon the number of his wives. "Manual labour among savages," says Westermarck, "is undertaken chiefly by the women; and as there are no day-labourers or persons who will work for hire, it becomes necessary for any one who requires many servants to have many wives." *There are no day-labourers or persons who will work for hire.* Women, then, are the first victims of that deep-rooted and instinctive preference for living by the labour of other people, which has played so momentous and sinister a rôle in the world's history. Among tribes whose mode of life has made them exploitable by stronger and more highly organized hordes—as, for example, an agricultural people which is conquered by a more mobile and disciplined tribe of herders—there, among the expropriated class, are day-labourers and people who will work for hire, for these have no choice or alternative; but among peoples where militant exploitation is impossible—as among the hunting-tribes—no man can be forced to work for another man, for the simple reason that there is no way of compelling him to share the product of his labour. But even here we see the economic phenomenon of the labour of women being exploited as the labour of man is exploited after conquest and the foundation of the exploiting State; and this is the case chiefly because certain natural disadvantages render them easily exploitable, as I shall show later.

It may be remarked in this connexion, that sexual division of labour appears to be quite arbitrary among primitive peoples; and that it often bears little resemblance to the division which has existed for so long among Europeans that it has apologists who regard it as being divinely ordained.[1] This suggests at least that the European division is arbitrary too. Indeed, it has undergone considerable change. Brewing, for example, was regarded as woman's work in mediaeval England. It is even supposed that the monasteries, which excluded

---

[1] Among the Chinese, for example, the woman never goes near the kitchen.

women from other service within their walls, employed women brewers. In general, it appears a fair conclusion that the occupations which are considered least desirable are given over to the subordinate sex. Thus men, according to the Vaertings, during the period when women dominated in Egypt, were forced to care for children and perform the drudgery of the household. Where military enterprise plays a part in tribal life, the division of labour appears to give validity to the contention of Spencer and others that man is militant and woman industrial; yet the exclusion of women from military activity is no doubt primarily due quite as much to the taboos against them as to their own lack of warlike spirit. Indeed, there are tribes where women take active part in fighting; and there are folk-tales in plenty which tell of their prowess—as, for example, in the epic lore of Greece and Russia. But because of a primitive awe of the function of menstruation, women are often considered unclean, and excluded on this account from many tribal activities, particularly from religious rites. Among such peoples, it would not be surprising to find that the same superstition excluded women from participation in any enterprise in which the tribal gods are so active and their aid so important as in war. In certain tribes of South Africa there is, according to Dr. Elsie Clews Parsons, a direct connexion between militancy and a taboo against woman. "A man sleeping with his wife must be careful not to touch her with his right hand. Otherwise his strength as a warrior goes from him and he will surely be killed."

Whatever be the basis of sexual division of labour among different tribes, and whatever minor differences there be in the relative position of the sexes, one thing is certain, and it is all we are at present concerned with, namely: in what Dr. Lowie has called "that planless hodge-podge, that thing of shreds and patches called civilization," woman almost invariably occupies a more or less inferior position. Dr. Lowie himself is careful to warn his readers against the popular assumption that the position of primitive woman is always abject, and that the status of woman offers a sure index of cultural advancement; nevertheless he says that "It is true that in by far the majority of both primitive and more complex cultures woman enjoys, if we apply our most advanced ethical standards, a less desirable position than man."

The obvious question is, Why? The answer is equally obvious, and has been so often stated and discussed that I need do no more than mention it here. Woman, however nearly her physical strength in the natural state may approximate that of man, is under a peculiar disadvantage in being the childbearing sex. During pregnancy, at least in its later stages, and during childbirth, she is powerless to defend herself against aggression. She is also at considerable disadvantage during the early infancy of her child. Man in the savage state, having none of that consideration which proceeds in a rough ratio with cultural development, takes advantage of her periodic weakness and her consequent need of protection, to force her into a subordinate position. Superstition, masculine jealousy and desire for domination, have of course been joined with the economic motive in bringing about this subjection to the male; but these motives could not have operated if her subjection had not been physically possible. If woman had had the natural advantage over man, she would have used it to subject him, precisely as he used his advantage to subject her; for the human being in the ruder stages exploits other human beings, when possible, as a matter of course, without any of those pretexts and indirections that characterize communities where the sense of human rights has become sufficiently general to gain the doubtful tribute of disingenuousness. It is among these more enlightened communities that the subjection of woman—or of any class—becomes reprehensible: a society that exploits human beings through ignorant brutality is not open to the same criticism as a society which continues to exploit them when clearly aware that in doing so it is violating a natural right.

II

So much for the cause of woman's subjection and exploitation. It has had powerful abetment in superstitious notions concerning sex, such as the primitive horror of menstruation. "Even educated Indians," says Dr. Lowie, "have been known to remain under the sway of this sentiment, and its influence in moulding savage conceptions of the female sex as a whole should not be underrated. The monthly seclusion of women has been accepted as a proof of their degradation in primitive communities, but it is far more likely that the causal sequence is to be reversed and that her exclusion from certain spheres of activity and consequently lesser freedom is the consequence of the awe inspired by the phenomena of periodicity."

It is evident that this superstition has operated powerfully to segregate women into a special class, excluded from full and equal participation in the life of the community. It is also reasonable to assume that it has stimulated the growth of many other superstitions that have hedged them about from time immemorial. It is probably, for example, closely connected with the Chinese association of evil with the female principle of the Universe, and with the Hebrew notion that sorrow entered the world through the sin of a woman. No doubt it may be connected with the mediaeval tendency to regard woman as a mysterious and supernatural being, either angelic or demoniac. The conception of sibyls and witches is derived from it; and likewise the notion which shows an interesting persistence even now, that a good woman is somewhat nearer the angels than a good man, and a bad woman much more satanic than a bad man.[1] Once

---

[1] According to news-reports on the day that this is written, Judge McIntyre of New York, sentencing a young woman in a criminal case, said: "When a woman is bad she is vicious and worse than a man, many, many times over."

the idea is established that woman is a being extra-human, minds prepossessed by this superstition may see her as either subhuman or superhuman; or these two notions may coexist, as in Christian society.

The notion that there is always a savour of sin in the indulgence of sexual appetite, even when exercised under due and formal regulation, has also had a profound effect on the status of women. This notion is to be found in both primitive and civilized communities; and since to each sex the other sex represents the means of gratifying sexual desire, the other sex naturally comes, where such a notion obtains, to represent temptation and sin. But where one sex is dominant and tends to regard itself as the sum of humanity, the other sex is forced to bear alone the burden of responsibility for the evil that sex represents; and it is therefore hedged about by the dominant sex with all sorts of restrictions intended to reduce its opportunities to be tempting, and thus to minimize its harmfulness.

It seems a fair assumption that the association of sin with sex-desire may have arisen from the antagonism between individual inclination and the domination of the group. Among peoples where the clan or the family is the final category, marriage is far from being exclusively a matter of individual interest and preference; indeed the individuals concerned may have little or nothing to say about it. The marriage is arranged by their elders, and the principals may not even see one another before their wedding day. Marriage under these conditions is a contract between families, an arrangement for founding a new economic unit and for perpetuating the tribe, as royal marriages are purely dynastic arrangements in behalf of a political order. Sexual preference can have little place in such a scheme; nothing, indeed, is more inimical to it. Love becomes an interloping passion, threatening the purely utilitarian basis upon which sex has been placed; and as such it must be discountenanced, and young men and women carefully segregated in order that this inconvenient sentiment may have no chance to spring up unauthorized between them.

In the Christian world this association of sin with the sexual appetite has prevailed since the days of St. Paul.[1] Sexual desire has been regarded as a

[1] It finds grotesque expression now and then. I remember seeing in a San Francisco newspaper a few years ago this headline: "Accused of having immoral relations with a woman other than his wife."

Woman's Status, Past and Present

base instinct, and its gratification under any circumstances as a kind of moral concession; therefore woman, as the instrument of sexual satisfaction in the dominant male, must be repressed and regulated accordingly, and to this end she was always to be under obedience to some man, either her husband or a male relative. "Nothing disgraceful," says Clement of Alexandria, "is proper for man, who is endowed with reason; much less for woman, to whom it brings shame even to reflect of what nature she is." Repression has combined with the proprietary idea to make chastity a woman's principal if not her only virtue, and unchastity a sin to be punished with a severity that, in another view, seems irrational and disproportionate, by permanent social ostracism, for example, as in most modern communities, or, as in Egypt and mediaeval Europe, by violent death. An extraordinary inconsistency appears in the fact that since Christian thought has chiefly connected morality with chastity, woman came to be regarded as the repository of morality, and as such to be considered on a higher moral plane than man. But it was really her economic and social inferiority that made her the repository of morality. She must embody the ideal of sexual restraint that her husband often found it inconvenient or onerous to attain for himself; and any unfaithfulness to this ideal on her part inflicted upon him a mysterious injury called "dishonour." He might indulge his own polygamous leanings with impunity, but his failure to make effective his sexual monopoly of his wife made him liable to contempt and ridicule. So strongly does this notion persist that one may find anthropologists, usually the most objective among our men of science, gauging the morality of a primitive people by the chastity of its women.

Of course the effect of the attempt to make the chastity of women a matter of morality and law, has been the precise opposite of the one aimed at. Society can never be made virtuous through arbitrary regulation; it can only be made unhappy and unamiable. The attempt to suppress all unauthorized expression of the sex-impulse in women tended to make them not only miserable and abject, but hypocritical and deceitful; and it tended also to make men predatory. This was its inevitable result in a society where women paid an exorbitant penalty for unchastity and men paid no penalty at all; a result which has made the relations between the sexes in the Christian world about as bad as any that could be imagined. Theoretically, to be sure, Christianity exacted of men the same degree of chastity as of women; practically it did no such thing, as may be amply proved even now by a study of the marriage and divorce laws of Christian nations, not excepting our own.[1] The sexual license of the dominant male was limited only by the practicable correspondence between his own desires and his opportunities; and thanks to that convenient being, the prostitute, his opportunities were plentiful. Hence for him, women were divided into two classes: the chaste and respectable from whom he chose the wife who kept his home, bore his children, and embodied his virtue; and those outcasts from society who promoted the chastity of the first class by offering themselves, for a price, as sacrifices to illicit sexual desire. Neither class was he bound to respect; for the only thing that compels respect is independence, and in neither the first nor the second class were women independent. From the man's point of view, such a social ar-

---

[1] In the State of Maryland, if the wife be found to have been unchaste before marriage, the husband is entitled to a divorce; but premarital unchastity on the part of the husband gives the wife no corresponding ground.

rangement was superficially satisfactory. It provided for what might be called the utilitarian ends of sex; that is to say, the man's name was perpetuated and his natural appetites gratified. But beyond this it left a good deal to be desired. Its worst effect was by way of a complete evaporation of the spiritual quality of union between man and woman and the very considerable dehumanization that in consequence set in. Both the wife and the prostitute were man's creatures *quoad hoc,* to be used for different purposes but equally to be used. It is hardly to be wondered at that man came to regard women as "the sex," and through his own management of their degradation came to feel and to express toward them a degree of contempt that cast considerable doubt on his own humanity. It is invariable that the person who is able to regard any class of human beings as *per se* his natural inferiors, will by so doing sacrifice something of his own spiritual integrity. In his relation to woman, man occupied a position of privilege analogous to that occupied by the aristocracy in the State; and he paid the same penalty for his exercise of a usurped and irresponsible power: a coarsening of his spiritual fibre. One of the oddest of the many odd superstitions that have grown out of male domination is the notion that men suffer less spiritual harm from sexual promiscuity than women; and this in spite of the biblical injunction, applied exclusively to their sex: "None who go unto her return again." This superstition is accountable for abundant and incurable misery; and so slow is it to disappear that one is inclined to advocate a movement for the emancipation of men, a movement to free them from the prejudices and prepossessions concerning women that are inculcated by the traditional point of view.

We have seen that the Christian philosophy looked upon woman as man's creature and his chief temptation, and that Christian society took good care to keep her in that position. In doing so, it made her the enemy of man's better self in a way that apparently was not foreseen by St. Paul, whose concern with the temptations of the flesh seems to have been a matter of more passionate conviction than his concern with those of the spirit. Woman's subordinate position; her enforced ignorance; the narrowness of the interests that were allowed her; the exaggerated regard for the opinion of other people that was bound to be developed in a creature whose whole life depended on her reputation—these conditions were calculated to evolve the sort of being which is hardly able to give clear recognition either to her own spiritual interest or to that of other people. Such a being would be the enemy of man's spiritual interest primarily through sheer inability to understand it. Public opinion was the arbiter of her own destiny; how could she be expected to conceive of any other or higher for man? Her whole life must be lived for appearances; how could she help man to live for actualities, and to make the sacrifice of appearances that such an ideal might entail? The only renunciation of the world that figured in her life was that which led to the convent; of that renunciation which involves being in the world but not of it—that steady repudiation of its standards which clears the way to spiritual freedom—of such a renunciation she would almost certainly be unable even to dream. The inevitable result of this enforced narrowness was well stated by John Stuart Mill in the essay which remains the classic of feminist literature; he pointed out that in a world where women are almost exclusively occupied with material interests, where their standard of appraisal is the opinion of other people, their ambition will naturally connect itself with material things, with wealth and prestige, no matter how inimical such an ambition may be to the spiritual interests of the men upon whom they depend. That there have been distinguished exceptions to this rule does credit to the strength of character which has enabled an individual now and then to attain something like spiritual maturity in spite of a disabling and retarding environment.

III

The effects of repression and seclusion on the character of woman have given rise, and an appearance of reason, to a host of other superstitions about her nature; notions which have been expressed in terms by many writers and have coloured the thought of many others. To offer a petty but interesting example, one of the most widely prevalent and most easily disproved of these is the belief that women are by nature more given to self-decoration than men. Certainly the practice in civilized society at present seems to bear out this notion. But when we turn to primitive communities we find, on the contrary, that the men are likely to be vainer of finery and more given to it than the women. The reason is simple: decoration of the person arises from the desire to enhance sex-attraction; and it is most industriously practised by that sex among whose members there is the keener competition for favour with members of the opposite sex. In European civilization marriage has been practically the only economic occupation open to women; but monogamous marriage, accompanied by an excess of females and an increasing proportion of celibacy among males, has made it impossible for every woman to get a husband; therefore the rivalry among them has been keen, and their interest in self-decoration has been largely professional. "If in countries with European civilization," says Westermarck, "women nevertheless are more particular about their appearance and more addicted to self-decoration than the other sex, the reason for it may be sought for in the greater difficulty they have in getting married. But there is seldom any such difficulty in the savage world. Here it is, on the contrary, the man who runs the risk of being obliged to lead a single life."

M. Vaerting, on this subject, takes the view that "the inclination to bright and ornamental clothing is dependent not upon sex, but upon the power-relation of the sexes. The subordinate sex, whether male or female, seeks ornament." But it would seem, in view of the accepted theory that self-decoration originates in the desire to enhance sex-attraction, that Westermarck's is the more reasonable explanation; moreover it covers certain cases in primitive life where the women, although their position is abject, nevertheless go plainly clad while the men are given to elaborate decoration of their persons.

In spite of all the evidence which anthropology arrays against it, however, the notion persists that woman is by nature more addicted to self-decoration than man; and there are not wanting advocates of her subjection, among them many women, who maintain that it shows the essential immaturity of her mind!

The notion that women are by nature mentally inferior to men, is primarily due to the fact that their enforced ignorance made them appear inferior. This is one of the strongest superstitions concerning women, as it is also one of the oldest. It has been much weakened by modern experience, but it has by no means disappeared. Indeed, it has stood in the way of dispassionate scientific study of the relative mental capacity of the sexes. Havelock Ellis, in his "Man and Woman," says that "the history of opinion regarding cerebral sexual difference forms a painful page in scientific annals. It is full of prejudices, assumptions, fallacies, over-hasty generalizations. The unscientific have a predilection for this subject; and men of science seem to have lost the scientific spirit when they approached the study of its seat. . . . It is only of recent years that a comparatively calm and disinterested study of the brain has become in any degree common; and even today the fairly well ascertained facts concerning sexual differences may be easily summed up." He then proceeds to show that those differences are few. It might be remarked here that such actual differences as appear are differences between man and woman as they now are, and can not be taken as final. If brain-mass, for example, depends to some extent on physical size and strength, the mass of woman's brain should tend to increase as she abandons her unnatural seclusion, engages in exacting occupations and indulges in vigorous physical exercise. Already there has been an astonishing change in the female figure. An interesting indication of this is a recent dispatch from Germany stating that according to the shoe-manufacturers of that country the average German woman of today wears a shoe two sizes larger than the woman of a century ago. If woman's body tends thus to enlarge with proper use, so in all likelihood will her brain.

Even Plato, who advocated the education of woman, held that while her capacities did not differ in kind from those of man, they differed in degree because of her inferiority in physical strength. It was a broad-minded view; for the most part women have simply been held to be by nature relatively weak-minded and therefore relatively ineducable. They have already passed one general test of educability, by entering schools on the same footing with men and showing themselves equally able to achieve a high scholastic standing; yet the Platonic notion persists that they are physically incapable of going as far as men can go in intellectual pursuits. This question can probably not be settled a priori to any one's satisfaction. It must be conceded, after the fact, however, that considering the short time that women have been tolerated in the schools and in the practical prosecution of intellectual pursuits, the showing they have made has really been quite as good as might reasonably be expected, and that it certainly has not been such as to warrant any arbitrary fixing of limits beyond which they can not or shall not go. Moreover, the physical weakness which is supposed to disable woman intellectually may be itself a result of her adaptation to her environment. There is no way that I know of to forecast with any kind of accuracy what a few generations of freedom will accomplish specifically in the way of spiritual development. Considering that human beings are "creatures of a large discourse," the matter is probably determinable only by experiment—*solvitur ambulando*.

Nor will there be any reason to agree with the numerous adherents of the idea that women are naturally incapable of great creative work in any field until they shall have failed, after generations and even centuries of complete freedom, to produce great creative work. This notion represents the last stand of a priori judgment concerning female intelligence. It is based on the theory, at present much in fashion, that men are more variable than women, and that both idiocy and genius are thus much more frequent in the male sex, while the intelligence of women tends to keep to the safe ground of mediocrity. The implications of this theory manifestly are that genius of the highest order can not be expected to appear in a woman. Since all cats are grey in the dark, according to the proverb, nothing worth saying can be said against this theory or for it. The data which underly it are simply incompetent and immaterial to any conclusion, one way or the other. They represent only a projection of men and women as they now are, and therefore can not be taken as a basis for speculation concerning men and women as they may become. To say, for instance, that because there has never been, to our knowledge, any woman, with the possible exception of Sappho, who showed the highest order of genius in the arts it is probable that there never can or will be, is much the same as to say that because there has never been a woman President of the United States no woman ever can or will be President. Let it be freely admitted that women have had opportunities in the creative field, and have fallen short of supremacy. What of it? One must yet perceive that the woman who has had those opportunities has been the product of a civilization constitutionally inimical to her use of them, and one may not assume that she has entirely escaped the effects of the continuous repression and discouragement exercised upon her by her social, domestic and political environment. When the power and purchase of this influence are fully taken into account, one would say it is not half so remarkable that women have missed supreme greatness in the arts as that they have been able to achieve anything at all. For in the arts, more than anywhere else, spiritual freedom is essential to great achievement; and spiritual freedom means a great deal more than the mere absence of formal restraint upon the processes of writing books or painting pictures. It is this important distinction that writers like Dr. Ellis and Dr. Hall, for example, have overlooked or ignored. They have simply failed to take into account the effect of a generally debilitating environment on the activities of the human spirit.

The environment of women has long been such as tends to make them, much more than men, the slaves of *"was uns alle bändigt, das Gemeine,"* and therefore to win release from the commonplace was, and still is, proportionately harder for a woman than for a man. The prevailing notion that a woman must at all costs cultivate the approval of the world lest she fail, through lack of it, to manœuvre herself successfully into the only occupation that society showed any cordiality about opening to her—this put a heavy premium on dissimulation and artifice. Women have not dared freely to be themselves, even to themselves. It was the effect of this constraint that Stendhal noted when he remarked that "the reason why women, when they become authors, rarely attain the sublime, . . . is that they never dare to be more than half candid."

It can not be gainsaid that the east wind of indifference which has chilled the fire of many a masculine artist who found himself part of an age indifferent to his order of talent, has always blown its coldest upon the woman who essayed creative work. The woman who undertakes to achieve artistic or intellectual distinction in a world dominated by men, finds herself opposed by many disabling influences. In an earlier day she had to endure being thought unwomanly, freakish, or wicked because she dared venture outside the limited sphere of sexuality that had been assigned to her. Now her presence in the field of spiritual endeavour is taken quietly; but she is constantly meeting with the tacit assumption, which finds expression in a thousand subtle ways, that her work must be inferior on account of her sex.[1] Again, the idea that marriage and reproduction constitute an exclusive calling and are really the natural and proper calling for every woman, still has general currency; and the very fact that a vast majority of women tacitly acquiesce in this idea, constitutes a strong pull upon the individual towards the orthodox and expected. Human beings are always powerfully drawn to be like their fellows; to be different requires a somewhat uncommon independence of spirit and toughness of fibre, and the fewer the individuals who attempt it, the more independence and tenacity it requires. "The fewer there be who follow the way to heaven," says the author of the Imitation, "the harder that way is to find."

The position of woman in creative work the world over is analogous to that of the man in America who ventures into the arts: he will be tolerated; he may even be respected; but he will not find in his

---

[1] As the only woman member of an editorial staff during a period of four years, I had ample opportunity for experience of this attitude. It was openly expressed only twice, both times, oddly enough, by women; but so universal was the unconscious assumption of inferiority that I may say without great exaggeration that it was only among my colleagues that I did not meet with it.

environment the interest and encouragement that will help to develop his talents and spur him to his best efforts. He may get sympathy and encouragement from individuals; but his environment as a whole will not yield what Sylvia Kopald has well termed the "tolerant expectancy" which nourishes and develops genius. In American civilization the prevailing ideal for men is business—material success; and our people retain, as Van Wyck Brooks has pointed out, the suspicious dislike and disregard which the pioneer community displays towards the individual whose governing ideals take a different line of development from those of his fellows. The artist, therefore, is likely to be looked upon as a queer being who loses something of his manhood by taking up purely cultural pursuits, unless and until, indeed, he happens to make money by it. Yet one never hears the intimation that because no Shakespeare or Raphael has ever yet appeared in this country, none ever will. Very well—imagine instead the prevailing ideal to be domesticity, and you perceive at once the invidious position of the woman artist in an exclusively or dominantly masculine civilization.

But what if the emergence of genius does not

depend so much on variability as upon the degree of spiritual freedom that the environment allows, and the amount and kind of culture that is current in it? "The number of geniuses produced in a nation," says Stendhal, "is in proportion to the number of men receiving sufficient culture, and there is nothing to prove to me that my bootmaker has not the soul to write like Corneille. He wants the education necessary to develop his feelings and teach him to communicate them to the public." The fact that prominent men of science accept the theory that genius is explained by variability, along with a number of conclusions which they have seen fit to draw from it, is no reason why their view should be considered final. Whole schools of scientists have before now gone wrong in the ticklish business of making speculative generalizations; they may go wrong again, for men of science are human, and may not be supposed to live wholly above the miasma arising from the stagnant mass of current prepossessions. So long as the apparent dearth of female genius may be satisfactorily accounted for on other grounds, one is under no compulsion to accept the theory that it is due to a natural and inescapable tendency toward mediocrity. When regarded fairly, indeed, this theory has something of an *ad captandum* character; it is not in itself disingenuous, perhaps, but it lends itself with great ease to an interested use. It offers strong support, for example, to an advocacy of an actual qualitative difference in the education of men and women. Women, being assumed to be fixed by nature at or below the line of mediocrity, shall be educated exclusively for marriage, motherhood, and the occupations which require no more than an average of reflective intelligence. This assumption underlies the educational plans of even such great libertarians as Thomas Jefferson and Theodore Hertzka; it represents a reversion, conscious or unconscious, to the primitive ideology which subordinates the individual to the group, taking for granted that the individual is to be educated not primarily for his or her own sake, but for an impersonal "good of society." Thus, whether they are aware of it or not, those who subscribe to this theory would not only keep in woman's way the discouraging postulate of inferiority that at present stands against her, but they would reinforce upon her those arbitrary limitations of opportunity to which her position of inferiority in the past may not unreasonably be ascribed.

IV

I have mentioned the repression of natural impulse inculcated upon women by their upbringing. This will probably not disappear entirely until the prevailing ideal in bringing up girls shall be to help them to become fully human beings, rather than to make them marriageable; for humanity and market-value have really little in common. For centuries the minds and bodies of women have been moulded to suit the more or less casual taste of men. This was the condition of their profession, which was to please men. Woman, in a word, got her living by her sex; her artificially-induced deformities and imbecilities had an economic value: they helped to get her married. It would be impossible to imagine a more profoundly corrupting influence than the dual ideal of sexuality and chastity that has been held up before womankind. "We train them up," says Montaigne, "from their infancy to the traffic of love." Yet men would have them, he says, "in full health, vigorous, in good keeping, high-fed and chaste together;[1] that is to say, both

---

[1] This was written, needless to say, before the casual taste of men set the fashion for women to be mincing and sickly.

hot and cold." The utter levity of this traditional attitude makes it fair to say that woman is man's worst failure. I know of no stronger argument for the social philosophy of the anarchist; for there is no more striking proof of the incapacity of human beings to be their brothers' keepers than man's failure, through sheer levity, over thousands of years to govern woman either for his good or her own.

With the growing disposition of women to take their interests into their own hands, this state of things is changing; but the curious superstitions to which its effect on the female character has given rise will long survive it. The world's literature, from the Sanscrit proverbs to the comic magazine of the twentieth century, is full of disparaging references to the character of women; to their frailty, their cunning, their deceitfulness, their irresponsibility, their treachery—qualities, all of them, which in a fair view they seem bound to have extemporized as their only defence in a social order which was proof against more honourable weapons. "A woman," says Amiel, "is sometimes fugitive, irrational, indeterminable, illogical and contradictory. A great deal of forbearance ought to be shown her, and a good deal of prudence exercised with regard to her, for she may bring about innumerable evils without knowing it." This is no doubt true, and the purposes of the moralist perhaps demand no more than a mere statement of the fact. But the critic's purposes demand that the fact should give an account of itself. Why does woman so regularly bear this character? Well, certainly the only life that European civilization offered to women in Amiel's day—the only views of life that it accorded them, the only demands on life that it allowed them—was a specific for producing the kind of creature he describes; and there is no doubt that it must have produced them by the million. The inference is inescapable that an equivalent incidence of the same educational and environmental influences upon men would have produced the same kind of men. The matter, in short, is not one of the primary or even the secondary character of women *qua* women or of men *qua* men; it is one of the effect of education and environment upon human beings *qua* human beings.

The effort to escape this inference gives rise to extraordinary inconsistencies in the current estimate of female character, and even the estimate put upon it by men of scientific habit. Women are supposed, for instance, to be tenderer and gentler than men—

"Tenderness," says Ellen Key, "distinguishes her whole way of thinking and feeling, of wishing and working"—yet they are also supposed to be more vengeful—"Hell hath no fury . . ." They are supposed to be creatures of impulse and sentiment —"*la femme, dont l'impulsion sentimentale est le seul guide écouté*" [1]—yet they are at the same time supposed to be calculating, particularly in their relations with men. Diluvial irruptions of sentimentalism are continually spewed over their nobility and self-sacrifice in the rôle of motherhood; yet men have taken care in the past to deny them guardianship of their own children. Schopenhauer, far on the right wing, again, appears to represent the legalistic point of view on this relation: he does not trust them in it beyond the first purely instinctive love for the child while it is physically helpless; he thinks they should "never be given free control of their children, wherever it can be avoided." Man, now, is more likely, he thinks, to love his child with a lasting love, because "in the child he recognizes his own inner self; that is to say his love for it is metaphysical [or egotistical?] in its origin." Occasionally, again, the world is treated to the diverting spectacle

[1] Elie Faure.

of some woman writer, like Dr. Gina Lombroso, trotting out all the poor old spavined superstitions and putting them through their paces in order to prove the strange contention that women are incapable of making the progress they have already made. Dr. Lombroso's ideal woman, as I have already remarked elsewhere in a review of her recent book, is something of a cross between an imbecile and a saint; that is to say, she conforms closely to the ideal which has been held up before the women of the Christian world; an ideal towards which millions of them have striven with a faithfulness which does more credit to their devotion than to their intelligence.

Since any discussion of woman's place in society must necessarily be to some extent a study in superstition, one can not really have done with superstition until one is done with the subject. It has seemed to warrant some special attention at the outset of this work not only because the past and present status of womankind can not be explained without reference to it, but because the future of womankind will in large measure depend upon the expeditiousness with which it and those prepossessions which spring from it, are laid aside. The sum of these superstitions and prepossessions may be expressed in the generalization that woman is primarily a function; and wherever any remote approach to this generalization may be discerned in a discussion of her status or her rights—as it may at once be discerned, for instance, in the sentimental side of the work of feminists as staunch as Ellen Key and Olive Schreiner—at just that point the abdication of the scientific spirit in favour of superstition may be suspected.

CHAPTER III

INSTITUTIONAL MARRIAGE AND ITS ECONOMIC ASPECTS

I

MARRIAGE, by a strictly technical definition, is a natural habit; that is to say, it is a relationship proceeding out of the common instinct of male and female to mate, and to remain together until after the birth of one or more children.[1] Organized society, on the other hand, always makes it a civil institution, and sometimes a religious institution. So long as man remained in the natural state, roaming about in search of his food as do the apes to-day, it may be supposed that marriage was based on personal preference and involved only the selective disposition of the individual man and woman and their common concern for the safety of their offspring. But as advancing civilization enabled mankind more easily to obtain and augment its food-supply, and consequently to secure greater

[1] Westermarck defines it as "a more or less durable connexion between male and female lasting beyond the mere act of propagation till after the birth of the offspring."

Institutional Marriage

safety and also to satisfy its gregarious instinct by living in numerous communities, the habit of marriage underwent a process of sanction and regulation by the group, and was thus transformed into a civil institution. While society remains ethnical, the family exercises supervision over the sexual relations of its members, but always subject to the approval or disapproval of the larger group—the tribe or clan. When the political State emerges, this function continues to be exercised by the family, but it is subject to sanction by the State and is gradually absorbed by it. Yet even where the State has usurped almost all the prerogatives of the family, custom continues to give powerful sanction to interference in marriage both by relatives and by the community.

Where the tribal religion takes on the form of ancestor-worship, or where much importance is attached to burial-rites, marriage and reproduction take on a religious significance. "As the dead," says Dr. Elsie Clews Parsons, "are dependent on the living for the performance of their funeral rites and sacrificial observances, marriage itself as well as marriage according to prescribed conditions, child-begetting and bearing, become religious duties.

Marriage ceremonial not infrequently takes on a religious character. Infanticide, abortion, celibacy other than celibacy of a sacerdotal character, and adultery, become sins. The punishment of the adulteress is particularly severe, although in some cases her value as property may guarantee her against punishment by death." [1]

Thus there may be, and in most civilized societies there is, a fourfold interference in marriage: interference by the family, by the community, by the State, and by the Church. An old Russian song had it that marriages were contracted

> By the will of God,
> By decree of the Czar,
> By order of the Master,
> By decision of the community,

—with not a word about the two persons immediately concerned. Nor is this strange, for marriage is not generally conceived of among either primitive or highly civilized peoples as a personal relationship. It is an economic arrangement, an alliance between families, a means for getting children. To allow so unruly a passion as love to figure

---

[1] E. C. Parsons: "The Family."

Institutional Marriage 59

in the selection of a mate, is an irregularity which may under certain circumstances be tolerated, but one which is nevertheless likely to be regarded with extreme disapproval. As individualism makes progress against group-tyranny, the preliminaries and the actual contracting of marriage become less the affair of God, the State, the family and the community, and more the affair of the two people chiefly interested; but once contracted, the marriage can hardly be said, even in the most civilized community, to be free of considerable regulation by these four influences. The time which Spencer foresaw, when "the union by affection will be held of primary moment and the union by law as of secondary moment," has by no means arrived. If the married couple be Roman Catholics, for example, they may not free themselves from an unhappy marriage without paying the penalty of excommunication; and if they live in a State dominated by the Catholic Church, they may be legally estopped from freeing themselves at all. Nor may they, save by continence, limit the number of their offspring without risking the same penalty. If they are Episcopalians or Lutherans they may divorce only on the ground of adultery, and the guilty party is forbidden to remarry. In communities where the influence of other Protestant sects predominates, and where, therefore, divorce and remarriage are not formally forbidden by the Church, the pressure of public opinion may yet operate to prevent them. The State not only prescribes the form that marriage shall take, but it may also either prohibit divorce—as in South Carolina, for example—or forbid it save in accordance with such regulations as it sees fit to make; and these regulations are not only of a kind that make divorce prohibitive to the poor, but they are often so humiliating as to constitute an effective barrier to the dissolution of unhappy unions. The State of New York offers an excellent illustration. Adultery is the only ground upon which divorce is allowed, and even then it may be refused if the action is taken by mutual consent. The couple who wish to be divorced must therefore, if there be no legal cause, go through the demoralizing business of making a case, which means that one or the other must provide at least the appearance of "misconduct"; and even then they are in danger of being found in collusion. But suppose one party to be giving legal ground; then the other party, in order to get proof, is obliged to resort to the lowest kind of espionage.

Such disreputable methods, however much they be in keeping with the nature and practices of the State, are hardly becoming to civilized society, and civilized persons are indisposed towards them. Their general effect is therefore to discourage application for divorce in New York and encourage it elsewhere.

It is significant of the unspiritual estimate generally put upon marriage, that incompatibility is rarely allowed as a legal ground of divorce. Violation of the sexual monopoly that marriage implies; prenuptial unchastity on the part of the woman; impotence; cruelty; desertion; failure of support; insanity; all of these or some of them are the grounds generally recognized where divorce is allowed at all. This is to say that society demands a specific grievance of one party against the other, a grievance having physical or economic consequences, as a prerequisite to freedom from the marriage-bond. The fact that marriage may be a failure spiritually is seldom taken into account. Yet there is no difficulty about which less can be done. Infidelity may be forgiven and in time forgotten; the deserter may return; the delinquent may be persuaded to support his family; the insane person may recover; even impotence may be cured. But if two people are out of spiritual correspondence, if they are not at ease in one another's society, there is nothing to be done about it. "Anything," says Turgenev, "may be smoothed over, memories of even the most tragic domestic incidents gradually lose their strength and bitterness; but if once a sense of being ill at ease installs itself between two closely united persons, it can never be dislodged." Modern society is slowly, very slowly, coming into the wisdom which prompted this observation. The gradual liberalization of the divorce-laws which our moralists regard as a symptom of modern disrespect for the sacredness of marriage, is in fact a symptom of a directly opposite tendency—the tendency to place marriage on a higher spiritual plane than it has hitherto occupied.

The State assumes the right either to allow artificial limitation of offspring or to make it a crime; and it exercises this assumption according to its need for citizens [1] or the complexion of its religious establishment. It also fixes the relative status and

---

[1] It is interesting in this connexion to note that in post-war England, where the thousands of unemployed workers constitute a heavy drain on the public purse and a baffling political problem, it has been made lawful to sell devices for birth-control. One now sees these devices conspicuously displayed in druggists' windows.

Institutional Marriage

rights of the two parties. In several American States, for instance, a married woman is incompetent to make contracts or to fix her legal residence. The Virginia law recognizes the primary right of the father to the custody of the child, yet it makes the mother criminally liable for the support of children. On the other hand, the husband is everywhere required by law to support his wife. Such laws, of course, like most laws, are felt only when the individual comes into conflict with them. The State does not interfere in many cases where married couples subvert its regulations—for example, the law which entitles the husband to his wife's services in the home and permits him to control her right to work outside the home, does not become binding save in cases where the husband sees fit to invoke it. As a rule the State forbids fornication and adultery.[1] In case of separation and divorce, if the parties disagree concerning financial arrangements or the custody of children, it exercises the right to arbitrate these matters.

The sanctions of interference by the family, save in the contracting of marriage by minors, are at

---

[1] In Maryland fornication is not a crime, although it may entitle a husband to divorce if he did not know of it at the time of the marriage. Adultery is punishable by a fine of ten dollars.

present those of custom, affection, and (in so far as it exists and may be made effective) economic power. When two persons have decided to marry, for instance, it remains quite generally customary for the man to go through the formality of asking the woman's nearest male relation for her hand. This is of course a survival from the period when a woman's male guardian had actual power to prevent her marrying without his consent. The influence of affection is too obvious to require illustration; it is the subtlest and most powerful sanction of family interference. Economic power is perhaps most commonly used to prevent or compel the contracting of marriage. It may make itself felt, where parents or other relatives are well-to-do, in threats of disinheritance if prospective heirs undertake to make marriages which are displeasing to them. A striking instance of the use of this power is the will of the late Jay Gould, which required each of his children to obtain consent of the others before marrying. It is not uncommon for legators to stipulate that legatees shall or shall not marry before a certain age under penalty of losing their inheritance.

These influences do not always, of course, take the same direction. At present, for example, arti-

Institutional Marriage

ficial limitation of offspring receives irregular but effective community-sanction in face of opposition by Church and State. Or again, public opinion almost universally condemns the idea that a father may, by his will, remove his children from the custody of their mother, although the State, as in Maryland and Delaware, may sanction such an act. But, however much they may check one another, these influences are all constantly operating to restrict and regulate marriage away from its original intention as a purely personal relationship, and to keep it in the groove of economic and social institutionalism. The reasons for this are to be found in the vestigiary fear of sex, love of power, love of the habitual, religious superstition, and above all in the notion that the major interests of the group are essentially opposed to those of the individual and are more important than his. A combination of two of these motives has recently come under my own observation in the case of a young woman whose parents can not forgive her for having divorced a man whom she did not love and married a man whom she did. They were accustomed to their first son-in-law, and resent the necessity of adjusting themselves to the idea of having a new one. Moreover, they feel that their daughter should have spared them the "disgrace" of a divorce. The fact that she was unhappy in her first marriage and is happy in her second seems to have little weight with them. They did their best to prevent her second marriage and are at present exerting every effort to make it unsuccessful. It is needless to emphasize the fact that this order of interference can not be expected to disappear while the notion persists that the actions of one adult member of a family or group can possibly reflect credit or discredit upon all the other members.

II

If one be an apologist for the present economic and social order, there is little fault to be found with this endless and manifold regulation of the most intimate concern of the individual, save that it is not as effective as it once was. Society, we are being constantly reminded, is founded in the family. No one, I think, will quarrel with this statement, particularly at this stage of the world's rule by the exploiting State. Marriage is, to quote Dr. E. C. Parsons, "an incomparable protection of society—

as society has been constituted"; and this for a reason which Dr. Parsons did not mention. Nor has the reason been stated by anyone else, so far as I am aware, although the fact is emphasized often enough. It is emphasized, however, largely in the spirit of a contemporary French writer who declares that "an institution upon which society [1] is based should not be represented to society as an instrument of torture, a barbarous apparatus. We know, on the contrary that this institution is good, and that it would be impossible to conceive of a better one upon which to base our customs." Well, but suppose it *is* an instrument of torture, or at least that we have come to find it highly unsatisfactory; must we, in spite of the fact, resolve to think it good because society is based upon it? Ought we not,

[1] It is important to call attention to the loose use of the word "Society" in this quotation, as practically synonymous with the State. In their final definition, the two terms are antithetical. There is general agreement among scholars, according to Professor Beard, that in the genesis of the State, exploitation was primary, and organization for other purposes, e. g., what we know as "law and order," was incidental and secondary. The term Society, then, really implies the disappearance of the State, and is commonly so used by scholars. Even now, too, tribes which have never formed a State and are without government of any kind, maintain society, i. e., a quite highly organized mode of communal life. Thomas Jefferson remarked this phenomenon among the American Indian hunting tribes, and so did the historian Parkman.

rather, to examine the order of society that institutionalized marriage helps to perpetuate, in order to determine whether it is worth preserving at the cost of preserving also an institution which has become "an instrument of torture"?

The reason why marriage is "an incomparable protection to society" lies in the fact that the continuance of the power of the exploiting State depends upon the relative helplessness of its exploited subjects; and nothing renders the subject more helpless against the dominance of the State than marriage. For monopoly, under the protection of the State, has rendered the support of a family extremely difficult, by closing free access of labour to natural resources and thus enabling the constant maintenance of a labour-surplus. Where there is little or no land not legally occupied, access to the soil is impossible save on terms that render it, if not downright prohibitive, at least unprofitable. The breadwinner who has neither land nor capital is thus forced to take his chance in a labour-market overcrowded by applicants for work who are in exactly his position: they are shut out from opportunity to work for themselves, and obliged to accept such employment as they can get at a wage deter-

Institutional Marriage 69

mined not by their capacity to produce, but by the number of their competitors. Not only is the wage-earner thus obliged to content himself with a small share of what his labour produces; he is forced to pay out of that share further tribute to monopoly in most of the things he buys. For shelter, for the products of the soil and mines, he pays tribute to the monopolist of land and natural resources; for industrial products, in most countries, he pays to the monopoly created by high tariffs. Or he may have to pay to both, as in the case of the purchaser of steel products.

Such disadvantages tend not only to keep wages near the subsistence-level, but to keep opinions orthodox—or if not orthodox, unexpressed. For the wage-earner gets his living on sufferance: while he continues to please his employer he may earn a living, however inadequate, for himself and family; but if he show signs of discontent with the established order, by which his employer benefits or thinks he benefits, he is likely to find himself supplanted by some other worker whose need makes him more willing to conform, in appearance at least. There are even conditions under which his mere unorthodoxy may bring him to jail, in thirty-four

States of this enlightened Republic. There are exceptional cases, of course, where his skill or special training makes him a virtual monopolist in his line and thus renders him indispensable, like a certain well-known professor who continues to hold his position in spite of his avowed economic unorthodoxy simply because there is no one else who can fill it. But it may be perceived at once that the average wage-earner with a family to support will be under much greater pressure to dissemble than will the worker who has no family; for where the single worker risks privation for himself alone, the married worker takes this risk for his family as well. Nor does economic pressure operate only towards the appearance of conformity; it operates towards actual conformity, for the person who has children to rear and educate will be strongly impelled towards conservatism by his situation. If he can get along at all under the present order, the mere *vis inertiae* will incline him to fear for the sake of his family the economic dislocation attendant upon any revolutionary change, and to choose rather to keep the ills he has.[1] Moreover, the unnatural situation popularly

[1] This motive is especially powerful in the United States, because monopoly in this country even now permits people to do relatively well. Moreover, there is still a strong current of optimism attrib-

called the "labour-problem," brought about through exclusion from the land, tends to create the psychology of the wage-slave: it tends to make people regard the opportunity to earn one's living not as a natural right, but as something that one receives as a boon from one's employer, and hence to accept the idea that an employer may be justified in dictating to his employees in matters of conduct and opinion.

Thus the economic conditions brought about by the State operate to make marriage the State's strongest bulwark; and those who believe that the preservation of the State, or of a particular form of it, is a sacred duty—their number among its victims is legion—are quite logical in taking alarm at the increasing unwillingness of men and women to

utable to the failure of Americans to see that the old days of almost unlimited opportunity ended with the closing of the frontier. If the American family finds itself in straitened circumstances, its members are likely to attribute the fact to "hard times," and to expect an improvement before long, since the country has recovered from a panic about every twenty years for the past century. They do not understand that the measure of recovery they hope for is now impossible. How many Americans, I wonder, have stopped to ask themselves why this country has suffered from *uninterrupted* economic "depression," with the exception of the war-period, ever since the panic of 1907? What they regard as depression is really the normal result of complete land-monopoly and high tariffs. Prices have continued to rise since the war; which is to say that real wages have fallen.

marry, or if they do marry, to have children. They are logical not only because marriage and children make for endurance of established abuses, but because, as I have already remarked, it is important for the State to have as many subjects as possible, to keep up a labour-surplus at home and to fight for the interests of its privileged class abroad; that is, so long as industry is able to meet the exactions of monopoly and still pay interest and wages. Where monopoly has reduced interest and wages to the vanishing-point, the State can no longer be said to be a going concern; its breakdown is then only a matter of time. This point has been reached in England, and hence the condition of which I have spoken: a numerous population is no longer desirable, for as unemployed they are a burden on the State and a menace to its existence. But as long as the State is a going concern, the Spartan rule is that best suited to its interests: obligatory marriage, and unlimited reproduction.

In modern civilization, however, in spite of the enormous power of the State, it would be extremely difficult if not impossible to enforce this rule. The State, with all its power, can not force its subjects to obey any law which they do not really want to obey

Institutional Marriage

—or perhaps I should say, which they want not to obey; and the growth of individualism has created a general distaste for any effort on the part of government to meddle directly in the affairs of citizens. Attempts to do so are likely to bring humiliation on the Government through its inability to enforce them, and to generate in the population a salutary disrespect for law; as the attempt to enforce the fourteenth and eighteenth Amendments has done in this country. With the decline of the patriarchal system, the contracting of marriage if not the status of marriage, is coming to be regarded as the exclusive concern of the individual. Many who would not for a moment tolerate compulsory marriage will tolerate a humiliating regulation of marriage; they will allow the State to make of marriage a life-long bondage, but they reserve the right to refuse to enter into bondage. The State may penalize celibacy by levying a special tax on unmarried persons; but it can no longer force people to abandon it.

Indeed, one may say without overmuch exaggeration that at present the preservation of marriage as an institution is almost solely due to its tenacity as an instinctive habit. For while marriage is the strongest bulwark of the State, the economic order for the sake of which the State exists tends nevertheless to discourage marriage because it progressively concentrates wealth in a few hands, and thus deprives the great mass of people of adequate means to rear and educate families. This condition is largely responsible for the fact that celibacy, illegitimacy and prostitution are on the increase in every civilized country; and that the average age at which marriage takes place tends steadily to become higher, as it takes longer to get into an economic position which makes possible the support of a family. In this connexion, Katharine Anthony's statement that factory-girls and heiresses are the country's youngest brides is significant. Neither the heiress nor the factory-girl has anything to gain by waiting: the heiress already has economic security and the factory-girl never will have it, for she and her husband—if she marries in her own class—will always be pretty much at the mercy of conditions in the labour-market. It should also be remarked that among the great middle class the standard of education for both sexes, but more particularly for women, is higher than among the very rich and the very poor; and this tends to advance the average age for marriage.

It tends as well to make children a heavy burden on the parents. Among primitive peoples, where difficulty in supporting a family is virtually unknown, where adjustment to the environment offers no complexities and childhood is therefore not so prolonged, and where, moreover, children through their labour become an economic asset, they are desirable.[1] But in a civilized society where the parental sense of responsibility has developed to the point where the child is reared for its own sake, where adaptation to the environment is a complex and lengthy process involving expensive education and prolonged dependence of the child upon the parents, and where the difficulty of getting a start in life tends also to lengthen the period of dependence; in such a society it is natural that the parental sense of responsibility should find expression in an artificial limitation of offspring to the number that the circumstances of the parents will enable them to educate properly. There is a further step that this feeling can suggest in these days of excessive eco-

[1] According to Herriot, children form the wealth of savage tribes.

nomic exploitation and ruinous wars; that is, refusal to reproduce at all: and this step an increasing number of married people are taking, to the great distress of self-appointed guardians of our customs and morals.

Failure to perceive the decisive importance of the connexion between the economic condition of the parents and the proper equipment of children for making their way in life often leads to absurd contradictions; as for example in that staunch friend of childhood, the late Ellen Key. No one is more insistent than this writer upon the importance of rearing the child for its own good; yet she gravely declares that "from the point of view of the nation, always from that of the children, and most frequently from that of the parents, the normal condition must be, that the number of children shall not fall short of three or four." Miss Key's primary failure is one that must be judged with great severity because it is both fundamental and typical —it pervades and vitiates the whole body of feminist literature. It is a failure in intellectual seriousness. Miss Key is fully aware of a persistent economic dislocation bearing on her thesis— "At present there is a shortage of labour for those willing to work, of

Institutional Marriage 77

food for the hungry, of educational advantages for those thirsting for knowledge, of nursing for the sick, of care for the children. The circumstances of the majority are now such as to produce, directly or indirectly, crime, drunkenness, insanity, consumption, or sexual diseases in large sections of the population." Again, "The struggle for daily bread, the cares of livelihood . . . are now the stamp of public as well as private life. . . . Married people have no time to cultivate their feelings for one another, . . . Through the cares of livelihood parents have no time to live with their children, to study them in order to be able really to educate them." [1] One must suspect a peculiar incapacity for logic in the writer who recognizes such conditions and still recommends three or four children as being the minimum number that people should have who wish to do their duty by their country, their children and themselves. Miss Key has been content to shirk inquiry into the fundamental cause of these conditions, and hence the means she recommends for their cure are silly and feeble. An international

---

[1] The first passage I have quoted is from "Love and Marriage"; the other two I have taken from Miss Key's "The Younger Generation," simply because I found the ideas they contain somewhat more clearly and definitely expressed in that book than in the other.

universal organization which is to regulate all competition and all co-operation; trade-unionism, the abolition of inheritances; the exercise of "collective motherliness" in public affairs; these are some of the means she offers for the regeneration of society. Probably never since the remark attributed to Marie Antoinette that if the starving populace could not get bread they should eat cake, has ineptitude gone further. If Miss Key's call to duty were brought to the attention of the well-to-do married couple of the city of New York whose means are sufficient to permit them to occupy an apartment of, let us say, two or three or four rooms, often without kitchen, they might agree with her in principle; but they would probably not attempt to bring up three or four children in such straitened surroundings and to educate them over a long span of years, for a very doubtful future. If this example seem special and far-fetched, I would remind my readers that over fifty per cent of people in this country are urban dwellers, and that the vast majority of them are worse off for dwelling space, not better, than the hypothetical couple I have cited.

It is, of course, among those who are worse off that children are most numerous. Ignorance and religious scruples—for the Church is strongest among the ignorant because of their ignorance—combine to produce large families among the class that can least afford them. For civilization, although it denies these people most things, grants them too great a fecundity. Among primitive peoples fecundity is decreased by various causes, such as excessively hard work, childbearing at a too early age, and prolonged lactation during which continence is often the rule. The average number of children borne by a savage does not often exceed five or six, whereas the civilized woman may bear eighteen or twenty, and it is not at all exceptional for the woman of our slums to bear ten or twelve. Among west-side women of New York whom Katherine Anthony questioned concerning frequency of pregnancies, one reported fifteen in nineteen years, another ten in twelve years, and another six in nine years. Obviously, then, when eugenists and moralists deplore what they term the modern tendency to race-suicide, they refer to the educated classes. The moralist argues from prepossession and may be dismissed from consideration; but the eugenist has scientific pretensions which are not without a certain degree of validity and can therefore not be lightly passed over. So long as he argues for improvement in the quality of the race through the substitution of intelligence for blind instinct in propagation, he is on solid ground: no one unprepossessed by the sentimentalism which regards legitimate children, however untoward be the circumstances of their birth and breeding, as a direct visitation from God, can deny that voluntary and intelligent attention to the quality of offspring offers better prospects for civilization than hit-or-miss quantity-production. The eugenist deplores the fact that at present this exercise of intelligence is confined to the comparatively small class of the educated and well-to-do, and that therefore the birth-rate among that class is all too small to offset the unchecked propagation of the ignorant and unfit. This is unfortunately true; and it suggests the obvious question: Why is there in every modern State so large a class of ignorant and unfit persons as to constitute a menace to the vitality of that State? If it is solely because the unfit are allowed to propagate unchecked, then those eugenists who advocate the sterilization of paupers and imbeciles and the encouragement of propagation among the intelligent classes by an elaborate system of State subsidy, may be listened to with respect if

Institutional Marriage 81

not with perfect faith in the practicability of their proposals. But how about that large mass of the physically and mentally normal who live at the subsistence-level, and whose progeny, if economic pressure tighten a little, are likely to be forced down into the class of underfed beings, dulled and brutalized by poverty, from whose ranks our paupers, imbeciles and criminals are largely recruited? To ignore the existence of this perennial source of unfitness is levity. To recognize it, and to assume that it results from over-propagation is to assume at the same time that the earth's population is too numerous for comfortable subsistence on the amount of cultivable land in existence. If this disproportion be real, the only hope lies in persuading this class to limit its offspring voluntarily to the number that the earth's surface will comfortably support. If it be only an apparent disproportion due to an artificial shortage of land created by monopoly, then the eugenist's program amounts simply to a recommendation that the population be somehow restricted to the number that can get subsistence on the terms of the monopolist. Henry George has conclusively disproved the validity of the Malthusian theory which underlies the assumption of over-population, while Oppenheimer's figures show that if land were freely available for use, the earth's present population might easily be supported on one-third of its arable surface.[1] Here, really, is the most convincing answer to the standard arguments for birth-control; yet so far as I know, the opponents of birth-control have never done much with it, whether out of ignorance or because of the profound economic readjustments that it implies. The eugenist, too, generally displays a constitutional aversion to attacking the problem of unfitness at the right end —which is, to inquire, first of all, why it exists. Hence the ineptitude of his proposals for social betterment: they would involve much unwieldy governmental machinery and considerably more intelligence than any State has ever displayed in dealing with social questions; and they would attack only the results of our social ills, leaving the causes freely operative.[2]

While those causes continue to operate, the support of a family, save in the comparatively small

---

[1] Franz Oppenheimer, Theorie der Reinen und Politischen Œkonomie. Berlin, 1912.

[2] For a striking and characteristic example of this ineptitude, I refer my readers to Dr. Havelock Ellis's little book, "Eugenics Made Plain."

Institutional Marriage 83

class of wealthy people, will be more or less of a burden. At present, this burden bears most heavily upon the middle-class man and the lower-class woman. Meretricious standards of respectability, among them the idea that a married woman must not work outside her home even when she is childless, tend to make marriage from the outset a burden on the man of the middle class. For it must be remembered that since the so-called feminine occupations have been taken out of the home, a man no longer gains an economic asset in taking unto himself a wife. Rather, he assumes a liability. This is especially true among the middle classes, where social standing has come to be gauged to some extent by the degree in which wives are economically unproductive. It is a commonplace in this country that women form the leisure class; and this leisure class of women, like leisured classes everywhere, has its leisure at the expense of other people, who in this case are the husbands. Moreover, it is among the middle classes that the standards of education are highest and the rearing of children therefore most expensive; and this burden is usually borne by the husband alone. Hence the emergence of the type of harassed *pater familias* at whom our comic artists poke much sympathetic fun, who meets his family now and then on Sundays, foots their bills, and is rewarded for his unremitting toil in their behalf by being regarded much in the light of a cash-register.

This sort of thing, of course, is not the invariable rule. There are many middle-class women who give their families untiring service, and an increasing number who, either from choice or necessity, engage in gainful occupations outside their homes. Of this country's eight and one half million women breadwinners, two million are married; and it may be assumed that a fair percentage of these are of the middle class. The great majority, however, are of the labouring class; and upon these, economic injustice weighs most heavily. It is these women who bear most children; and it is they who, when their husbands are unable or unwilling to meet the growing expenses of the family, assume the double burden of "woman's work" in the home and whatever they can get to do outside that will enable them to earn a few dollars a week, in order to "keep the family together." Miss Katharine Anthony, in her book, "Mothers Who Must Earn," gives a striking picture of the unskilled married women workers

Institutional Marriage 85

of west-side New York, victims of a crowded labour-market, who take the hardest jobs at the lowest pay, in order that they may give some few poor advantages to the children they have brought into the world unwillingly, knowing that they could not afford them. "The same mother," says Miss Anthony, "who resents the coming of children and resigns them so apathetically to death, will toil fourteen hours a day and seven days a week to keep up a home for the young lives in her charge."

Such testimony, and testimony of a similar kind from governmental investigators, somehow makes the general run of social criticism appear frivolous and superficial. The married wage-earner, worn with excessive childbearing, who still finds strength to work long hours in laundry or factory during the day and do her housework at night, hardly fits into the picture of selfish, emancipated women, wilfully deserting their proper sphere of domesticity either to seek pleasure or to maintain their economic independence. Indeed, the idea of economic independence is quite at variance with her notions of respectability. "Not to work," says Miss Anthony, "is a mark of the middle-class married woman, and the ambitious west-side family covets that mark.

Hence comes the attempt to conceal the mother's employment, if she has one, which is one of the little snobberies of the poor." The sole object of these women's toil is to preserve the home, chief prop of a social order which bears upon it with crushing weight; and their adherence to a social philosophy which regards the preservation of the home as peculiarly the business of women is evident in the fact that they contribute the whole of their meagre earnings to its upkeep, whereas their husbands are likely to contribute only as much of their own earnings as they see fit.

It goes without saying that the conditions I have cited have a profound effect on the psychology of parents, and therefore on the lives of children. The rearing of children, if justice is to be done them, is one of the most exacting tasks that can be undertaken. The adjustment that is required to fit parents to the personalities of their children and children to those of their parents and of one another, is in itself a most delicate and difficult process, and one upon which the nature of the child's adjustment to the larger world greatly depends. Such a process naturally involves friction, and therefore, if it is to be successful, calls for no little tact and patience in the parents; and cramped quarters, sordid poverty, and exhausting labour are hardly conducive to the possession of either of these qualities. Children of the middle class, it is remarked often enough, hardly know their harassed, overworked fathers; but children of the labouring class are likely to know neither of their parents, or to know them only as fretful, quarrelsome people, brutalized by overwork. "The strain of bringing up a family on the average workingman's wage," says Miss Anthony, "reduced as this is likely to be by unemployment, sickness, or drink, constitutes, indeed, the dark age of the tenement mother's life. It is not strange that the good will existing between husband and wife often gives way beneath it. 'I tell my husband,' said Mrs. Gurney, 'it's not right for us to be quarreling all the time before the children. But it seems like we can't help it. He's so worried all the time and I'm so tired. If we were easy in our minds we wouldn't do it.'"

Nor do the children of these people have anything much better to look forward to than such a lot as that of their parents, for poverty drives them too into the labour-market as soon as they are old enough to earn, to the profound distress of reformers who refuse to face the basic question of child-labour, namely: whether it is better for human beings, even if they be children, to work for their living or to starve. This applies not only to the children of our industrial labouring classes, but to those of the agricultural labourer and the tenant-farmer, who pay the same penalty for the exploitation of their parents. There is no little irony in the fact that our growing consciousness of the right of children to be well born and well reared proceeds hand in hand with an economic injustice which renders it impossible to secure that right for all children.

If responsibility for the upbringing of children is to continue to be vested in the family, then the rights of children will be secured only when parents are able to make a living for their families with so little difficulty that they may give their best thought and energy to the child's development and the problem of helping it to adjust itself to the complexities of the modern environment. Such a condition is not utopian, but quite possible of attainment, as I shall show later. But for the present, and for some time to come, marriage and parenthood will continue to make men and women virtual slaves of the economic order which they help to perpetuate. Small wonder that the women of whom Miss Anthony writes are thoroughly disillusioned concerning "marriage life," and would avoid it if they "had it to do over." Marriage as an institution has little to offer these people save toil and suffering; it is, as I have remarked, its tenacity as an instinctive habit that makes them its victims. And if it were not for the responsibilities that marriage entails, responsibilities which make people fearful of the economic uncertainty involved in revolutionary change, the economic order that makes marriage "an instrument of torture" and thwarts the development of children, would not last overnight.

Both as a personal relationship and as an institution, marriage is at present undergoing a profound modification resulting from the changing industrial and social position of women. The elevation of woman from the position of a chattel to that of a free citizen must inevitably affect the institution in which her subordinate position has been most strongly emphasized—which has been, indeed, the chief instrument of her subordination. The woman who is demanding her rightful place in the world as man's equal, can no longer be expected to accept without question an institution under whose rules she is obliged to remain the victim of injustice. There is every reason therefore, assuming that the process of emancipation shall not be interrupted, to expect a continuous alteration in the laws and customs bearing on marriage, until some adjustment shall be reached which allows scope for the individuality of both parties, instead of one only. The psychological conflict involved in the adaptation of marriage to woman's changing position and the changing mentality that results from it, is not to be underrated. At present the process of adjustment is needlessly complicated and this attendant conflict immensely exaggerated, by an economic injustice which bears most heavily on married people. Individualism is developing in modern society to such an extent that marriage based on anything but affection seems degrading; but economic injustice is progressing simultaneously with such strides that marriage based on nothing but affection is likely to end in disaster; for affection and the harassment of poverty are hardly compatible. If this complication were removed, as it could be, we should probably find that the adjustment of marriage to shifting ideals and conditions would come about in a natural and advantageous manner, as adjustments usually do when vexing and hampering conditions are removed. The question will settle itself in any case. Just how, no one, of course, can tell; but however revolutionary the adaptation to new conditions may be, it will not *seem* revolutionary to the people of the future because "the minds of men will be fitted to it." This is an all-important fact, and one that is too little respected; for the desire to enforce our own moral and spiritual criteria upon posterity is quite as strong as the desire to enforce them upon contemporaries. It is a desire which finds a large measure of fulfilment—where is the society which does not struggle along under a dead weight of tradition and law inherited from its grandfathers? All political and religious systems have their root and their strength in the innate conservatism of the human mind, and its intense fear of autonomy. Because of this conservatism, people never move towards revolution; they are pushed towards it by intolerable injustices in the economic and social order under which they live. There were, and are, such injustices in the laws and customs of the Christian world governing marriage and the relations of the sexes; hence the changes which have already begun, and may conceivably proceed until they shall prove as far-reaching as those by which marriage in the past was transformed from an instinctive habit into an institution subject to regulation by everyone except the two people most intimately concerned.

CHAPTER IV

WOMAN AND MARRIAGE

I

PERHAPS the most pronounced conventional distinction between the sexes is made in their relation to marriage. For man, marriage is regarded as a state; for woman, as a vocation. For man, it is a means of ordering his life and perpetuating his name, for woman it is considered a proper and fitting aim of existence. This conventional view is yielding before the changing attitude of women toward themselves; but it will be long before it ceases to colour the instinctive attitude of the great majority of people toward women. It is because of the usual assumption that marriage is woman's special province, that I have discussed its general aspect somewhat at length before considering its relation to women in particular. This assumption, I may remark, has been justified expressly or by implication by all those advocates of freedom for women who have assured the world that woman's "mission" of wifehood and motherhood would be better fulfilled rather than worse through an extension of her rights. If we imagine the signers of the Declaration of Independence, in place of proclaiming the natural right of all men to life, liberty, and the pursuit of happiness, arguing with King George that a little more freedom would make them better husbands and fathers, we shall imagine a pretty exact parallel for this kind of argument on behalf of the emancipation of women.

The belief that marriage and parenthood are the especial concern of women is rooted in the idea that the individual exists for the sake of the species. Biologically, this is of course true; but it is equally true of male and female. Among primitive peoples, where individuation has not progressed as far as among more highly civilized peoples, this idea still prevails in regard to both sexes. Among these peoples the man who must remain unmarried and childless is considered quite as unfortunate as the woman who suffers the same fate. Among civilized peoples, on the other hand, where individuation has progressed farthest, it is not usual to look upon the male as existing solely for the species; but it is usual for the female to be so regarded, because, having had less freedom than the male, she has not been able to assert to the same extent her right to live for herself. The one-sided view that the future of the race depends solely on women has curious results: a nation may send the best of its male youth to be destroyed in war without overmuch anxiety being manifested in any quarter over the effect of this wholesale slaughter upon future generations; but if the idea of enlisting women in military service be so much as broached, there is an immediate outcry about the danger to posterity that such a course would involve. Yet it requires only a moderate exercise of intelligence to perceive that if there must be periodic slaughter it would be better, both for the survivors and for posterity, if the sexes were to be slaughtered in equal numbers; and more especially is this true, for obvious reasons, where monogamy is the accepted form of marriage. Again, although it is extremely hard to get laws passed to protect men from the hazards of industry, the laws designed to protect women—*i. e.*, posterity—which have been passed at the instance of reformers and social workers, already constitute a serious handicap to women workers in their necessary competition with men in the labour-market.

Yet every child must have two parents, and certainly unfitness or disability in the father must have a bad effect upon his offspring, even though it be less harmful than unfitness or disability in the mother.

The view of woman as a biological function might be strongly defended on the ground of racial strength if that function were respected and she were free in discharging it. But it is not respected and she is not free. The same restrictions that have kept her in the status of a function have denied her freedom and proper respect even in the exercise of that function. Motherhood, to be sure, receives a great deal of sentimental adulation, but only if it is committed in accordance with rules which have been prescribed by a predominantly masculine society. *Per se* it is accorded no respect whatever. When it results from a sexual relationship which has been duly sanctioned by organized society, it is holy, no matter how much it may transgress the rules of decency, health, or common sense. Otherwise it is a sin meriting social ostracism for the mother and obloquy for the child—an ostracism and an obloquy, significantly enough, in which the father does not share.

The motives behind the universal condemnation

of extra-legal motherhood are various and complex; but I believe it is safe to say that the strongest is masculine jealousy. Motherhood out of wedlock constitutes a defiance of that theory of male proprietorship on which most societies are based; it implies on the part of woman a seizure of sexual freedom which, if it were countenanced, would threaten the long-established dominance of the male in sexual matters, a dominance which has been enforced by imposing all manner of unnatural social and legal disabilities upon women, such, for example, as the demand for virginity before marriage and chastity after it. The woman who bears an illegitimate child violates one of these two restrictions. On the other hand, the man who begets an illegitimate child violates no such restriction, for society demands of him neither virginity nor chastity; therefore he is not only not punished by social ostracism, but he is often protected by law from being found out.[1]

The fact that paternity may so easily be doubtful furnishes a strong motive for the attempt to enforce

[1] Code Napoléon: *"La recherche de la paternité est interdite."* This provision was expunged in 1913. In Massachusetts, the father's name may not be given in the record of birth except on the written request of both father and mother. No similar protection against publicity is provided for the mother.

chastity upon women; but that this is not so potent as the idea of male proprietorship is evident from the practice which exists in many primitive societies, and appears formerly to have existed in Europe, of lending wives to visitors, as a mark of hospitality. Adultery thus imposed on a woman by her husband is not only regarded as quite proper, but the children that may result are considered his legitimate offspring. The superstitious notion that a woman's honour is a matter of sex, and that she can not be considered virtuous if her sex-life is not conducted in accordance with regulations imposed by organized society, also has something to do with the disgrace that attaches to illegitimate motherhood; but of course this superstition itself has its source in masculine dominance. Indeed, there is no need to emphasize the fact that the whole mass of taboo and discrimination arrayed against the unwedded mother and her child is the direct result of the subjection of women; for in a society where women dominated— or even where they were the equals of men—illegitimacy would either not exist at all, or its consequences would be made to bear either upon the father or upon both parents equally. This may seem an extravagant statement in view of the harshness with which women themselves are prone to treat the unmarried mother. But it should not be forgotten that women are what the procrustean adaptations of a factitious morality have made them. They have been taught to believe that motherhood out of wedlock is a cardinal sin, and the value and fragility of reputation have been effective hindrances to any impulse of lenience toward the sinner. Their attitude, moreover, has been tinged with a feeling that may be termed professional. Marriage has been, generally speaking, the only profession open to them; their living and their social position have depended on it, and still do in great measure; therefore the woman who commits a sexual irregularity acts unprofessionally, somewhat as the trader who smuggles wares into a tariff ridden country and undercuts his competitors. The position of the unmarried mother is analogous to that of the married mother in certain societies of which I have already spoken, whose children are considered illegitimate because she has not been bought. Even the prostitute, although she is a social outcast, is sooner tolerated, because while prostitution, like marriage, has been established on a commercial basis, it is a non-competing institution. It does not impair the economic value of the "virtuous" woman's chief asset. Prostitution is condoned as a protective concession to the postulated sexual needs of men; the prostitute has been justified, and even praised in a back-handed way, as "the most efficient guardian of virtue";[1] that is to say, of the arbitrary restraints on women which pass for virtue in a society where woman is the repository of morality. Illegitimacy, on the other hand, or at least that large share of it which implies a fall from conventional virtue, is an embarrassing suggestion of sexual need in woman. Therefore, it is a disturbing phenomenon, intimating as it does to virtuous women that the duplex morality to which their freedom is sacrificed is unnatural and unworkable.

There is a sense, of course, in which extra-legal motherhood is, if not sinful, at least unjust. The mother knows that the child she bears out of wedlock will be forced, although innocent, to share with her in the world's displeasure at her defiance of conventional taboo, and that the sneers of its legitimately born playmates may have a blighting effect upon its spiritual development. She knows also, unless she be well-to-do or especially well qualified

---

[1] Lecky, "History of European Morals." Chapter V.

to earn, that her child will be at a disadvantage from the start in the matter of livelihood and education unless the father be willing—or required by law—to contribute to its support. There is likely to be a grim consistency in legal injustices. Sometimes the denial of one right makes expedient the denial of another, as when the poor, having been reduced by legalized privilege to want and squalor, are legally deprived of the alcohol with which they increase their wretchedness in an attempt to find forgetfulness of their misery. The denial to women of economic opportunity has made expedient denial of freedom in performing the function of motherhood. Men, having enjoyed a virtual monopoly of earning power, have been regarded as the natural providers for women and children; therefore a woman has been required to get a legal provider before she could legally get a child; and if one accepted her legal disabilities without questioning their justice, this restraint might appear quite justifiable. This may be taken as an argument for weakness or wantonness in the unmarried mother. If so, it must certainly apply with equal force to the unmarried father—with double force indeed, for he knows that his act will not only add to the difficulties, numerous enough under the best circumstances, that his child will have to contend with, but that it means social ostracism for the mother. Thus every illegitimate child, as society is at present constituted, is the victim not only of social but of parental injustice.

It is hardly necessary to discuss further the economic aspects of the question. In a society where economic opportunity is pretty well monopolized by men, the task of the mother with children to support is, as I have shown in the preceding chapter, extremely difficult; and it may even be rendered impossible where the disgrace of unmarried motherhood decreases such comparatively slight opportunity as industry, even now, offers a woman. The effect of this disability shows clearly in any comparison of the death-rates among legitimate and illegitimate babies. The rate among illegitimate children is often twice as high as that among children born in wedlock. Truly marriage is an invaluable protection to motherhood and childhood in a society which denies them any other.

Instead of joining in the universal condemnation of illegitimacy, it seems more reasonable to question the ethics of a society which permits it to exist.

Certainly no social usage could be more degrading to women as mothers of the race than that which makes it a sin to bear a child; and nothing could be more grotesquely unjust than a code of morals, reinforced by laws, which relieves men from responsibility for irregular sexual acts, and for the same acts drives women to abortion, infanticide, prostitution and self-destruction. I know of no word that may be said in justification of such a code or of a society that tolerates it. As marriage ceases to be a vested interest with women, and as their growing freedom enables them to perceive the insult to their humanity that this kind of morality involves, they will refuse to stand for it. Those who prefer to regard woman as a function will devote their energy to securing conditions under which she may bear and bring up children with a greater degree of freedom and self-respect than conventional morality allows her. As for those who prefer to regard her as a human being, they will naturally demand the abolition of all discriminations based on sex; while all women must certainly repudiate the barbarous injustice of organized society to the illegitimate child.

This is hardly to be regarded as a prophecy, for the revolt has already begun. A small minority of women in Europe have for some time been denouncing this injustice, the most prominent among them being the famous Swedish champion of childhood, Ellen Key. Their influence has already been reflected in the laws of several countries. In Scandinavia, in Switzerland, and even in France, laws have already been enacted either removing or modifying the legal disabilities of the child born out of wedlock, and fixing the responsibilities of the father. There are similar laws in Australia and New Zealand. These laws vary in scope, but their general tendency is toward the abolition of illegitimacy and recognition of joint parental responsibility for every child brought into the world. In this country, where unjust legal discriminations against unmarried mothers and their children are still in force, the Woman's Party is demanding laws recognizing every child as legitimate, and determining the responsibilities of unmarried parents. The abolition of illegitimacy will naturally mean that the child of unmarried parents will have the same right to the father's name, and to support and inheritance, as the child born in wedlock.

There is a general impression, to which I have adverted, that marriage is a great protection to women. Bachofen and his followers even went so far as to suppose that she herself originally devised it for that purpose. This school quite overlooked the fact that in so far as it has been a protection it has been so only because society has been inimical to her interests, and has allowed her no other defence against itself. Marriage has certainly not protected her in the past from hard labour, cruelty, and mental and spiritual deterioration. In spite of these well-known facts, the notion persists that it is of inestimable benefit to her; and those influenced by this superstition are likely to fear that to abolish illegitimacy, with its humiliating consequences, will be to encourage "free love" and thus to expose women to victimization by unscrupulous men. Such a view not only carries an untenable assumption of feminine inferiority, but it carries an equally untenable assumption that marriage constitutes a protection against victimization by unscrupulous men. Not only did our marriage-laws until recently give a woman into the absolute power of her husband, however unscrupulous he might be, but they left her no way of escape. On the other hand, they protected the husband's sexual monopoly of his wife and his right to be considered the only legal parent of their children. Indeed, the law has gone further; it has exposed women to victimization by protecting men from detection in illegitimate parentage. Laws equalizing the responsibilities of men and women towards illegitimate children, will reduce temptation to unscrupulous conduct, for men will be aware that if it result in the birth of a child they will be obliged to acknowledge their parenthood and assume the attendant responsibilities.

I might remark here that some communities have tried to deal with this question in what seems to me a very bungling manner, namely: by forcing the "seducer" of a woman under the legal age of consent to choose between marrying her and going to jail. Such laws represent concessions to traditional prejudices, and have little relation either to justice or common sense. They take no cognizance of the inclination of the parties or their fitness for marriage; hence they afford a stupid way of legitimizing the child. It would be much more sensible to regard every child as legitimate by the very fact of having arrived in the world, and to demand of its parents a full discharge of parental responsibility, without complicating it with the very different question of marital obligations. Another legal provision which is as general as it is humiliating to women is that which permits a father to recover damages from the seducer of his daughter. This law, which is in force in several of our States, is supposed to find justification in the daughter's status as a servant in her father's house; but since the law grants him no similar redress for the seduction of a servant who is not his daughter, it is evident that its real basis is in a surviving notion of woman as the natural property of a male owner. These laws do not lessen the disgrace that attaches to extra-legal birth; rather they recognize and endorse it.

The importance of abolishing illegitimacy is not to be underrated, for it means the removal of the legal sanctions which have enforced a barbarous custom. But the abolition of illegitimacy can not be expected entirely to remove the stigma attaching to unmarried motherhood and birth out of wedlock. That will disappear only when the economic independence of women shall have resulted in a spiritual independence which will lead them to examine critically the social dogmas that have been forced upon them, and to repudiate those which conflict with justice. In other words, it will involve an adaptation to more humane ethical standards; an adaptation which has begun but may be long in reaching completion, for superstition and taboo are not easily eradicated.

II

The assumption that justice to motherhood and childhood will undermine the institution of marriage implies that marriage as an institution is based on injustice; which is to assume that it is fundamentally unsound. That it does, under present economic conditions, involve serious injustice to both sexes I have shown in the preceding chapter. But this notion implies something more: it implies that marriage is acceptable to women only or chiefly because it offers them a position of privilege—the privilege of exemption from the social and economic consequences of illegitimate motherhood. There is some show of reason in this; for the disabilities which marriage puts on women are in most communities humiliating and onerous, more particularly since the unmarried woman has so generally succeeded in establishing her right to be treated as a free agent. The abolition of illegitimacy may conceivably undermine institutional marriage; yet hardly before women are economically free. For her need of society's protection against itself in the discharge of her maternal function has certainly had less to do with woman's long acquiescence in the disabilities which marriage involves than the fact that marriage offered the only career which society approved for her or gave her much opportunity to pursue. She was under enormous economic and social pressure to accept those disabilities, and she yielded, precisely as thousands of men who have been under analogous pressure to get their living under humiliating conditions, have yielded, rather than not get it at all.

Since we have been discussing unmarried motherhood, we may appropriately begin our consideration of these disabilities by examining the status of motherhood in marriage. The married mother, particularly in modern times, is the object of a sickly pawing and adulation and enjoys a certain formal respect—not, however, as a mother, but as a mother of legitimate children. While she continues to live with her husband, she may exercise considerable supervision over the rearing of her offspring; indeed in some communities she is, by force of custom, supreme in this province. But in case of separation or the death of her husband, she may find herself without any legal claim to their guardianship or custody, for until recently children born in wedlock have been generally held to belong exclusively to the father. The principle of joint guardianship is coming to be recognized in modern jurisprudence, but there are communities where the old laws still hold. In Virginia, for example, the father's claim is always preferred to that of the mother. In Maryland and Delaware it is preferred to such an extent that he may even, by his will, deprive her of the guardianship and custody of her children after his death. This provision is a survival from English common law, and is a logical correlative of woman's status under that law, which was that of a minor. Her position with regard to her children was one of responsibilities with no compensating rights; and although the discriminations against her have been modified here and there, this is still pretty generally her position. In this respect the unmarried mother is better off than the mother of legitimate children, for in most countries, as the only legal parent of her child, she exercises the right of guardianship and control and possesses full claim to their services and earnings. The unmarried mother, in a word, bears her own children; the married mother bears the children of her husband.

Usage, as every one knows, is far ahead of the laws governing the rights of the married mother. In France, where her legal position is notoriously bad, her relation to her family is nevertheless one of influence and authority. In this country also her actual position is generally far better than that allowed her by the law. But this is merely to say that most husbands are more humane than the law; and the fact may not be ignored that so long as legal discriminations bar her from an equal share with her husband in the control and guardianship of her children, she exercises parental rights only on sufferance. It is the law which finally fixes her status in this as in other matters; and as long as she may legally be made to suffer injustice on account of her sex, she can hardly be called her husband's equal, no matter what privileges she may enjoy by virtue of his indulgence.

So much for the disabilities of the married mother. Her compensations are the immunity that marriage affords her from society's displeasure and consequent persecution; the inestimable advantage of her husband's co-operation in making a home for her children, and in rearing and educating them; and the fact that they have a legal claim upon him for support and inheritance.

Her own claim for support does not depend, in law, upon her motherhood, but upon her wifehood. She is entitled to support whether she has children or not. On the other hand the law, in most communities, allows her nothing more than mere support, while at the same time it maintains certain restrictions upon her economic independence. Although most States now allow the wife to control her own earnings in industry, her services in the home are still pretty generally her husband's property, and any savings that result from economy in her domestic management belong to him, and so does any money earned by her in her own house, as from taking in boarders or lodgers. In short, while she works in the home her status is that of her husband's servant.[1] He may even, as in Michigan, still prevent her from undertaking employment outside the

[1] A recent decision in the State of New York declared that a husband is not required to fulfil his promise to return money loaned him by his wife, when she has accumulated it through economy in her housekeeping; because every saving of the kind is the property of the husband, as are the services of the wife. The wife has no money of her own.

Woman and Marriage 113

home, simply by withholding his consent. Nor is this the only way in which the opportunities of a married woman are restricted. She is frequently disqualified by her status for engaging in business on her own account, or for doing so without her husband's consent. She may also be disqualified by law or prejudice for engaging in certain professions, such as teaching, an occupation in which, strangely enough, a married woman is frequently held to be incapable.

The claim for alimony which at present constitutes such a fecund source of injustice to men and corruption among women, implies the assumption that a woman is economically helpless, that she is a natural dependent whose support, having been undertaken by her husband, must be continued even after divorce, until she dies or finds another husband to support her. It does not take into account the woman's rightful claim to any property that she may have helped her husband to accumulate, for the question whether or not she shall receive alimony is within the discretion of the court. On the other hand, the awarding of alimony may give a woman a claim to income from property possessed by her husband before marriage and therefore not rightfully to be enjoyed by her; it may, furthermore, give her an equally unjustifiable lien on his future earnings. Thus it allows women at once too little and too much. If the community is to continue to fix the economic obligations which marriage shall entail, it might be fairer to both sexes if those obligations were fixed as they have been in certain of our Western States. In those States, property acquired during marriage is regarded as common property, and in case of separation must be divided equally. Neither party may, during the marriage, dispose of such property without consent of the other; nor may either party dispose of more than half of it by will. On the other hand, either party has free disposal of property acquired before marriage, or inherited during marriage. In case one party dies intestate, the other shares equally with children in his or her half of the common property, and in other property. Thus the law raises woman above the status of a dependent and recognizes marriage as an equal partnership. Such laws, of course, do not fit all cases, for all marriages are by no means equal partnerships; but so long as the State insists upon maintaining a blanket-regulation of the marital relation, some such arrangement would seem to be more

Woman and Marriage 115

nearly just, both to men and women, than the laws now in force in most communities.

I have given only a partial list of the economic disabilities enforced upon a good many millions of married women. Their status in the various countries of the civilized world ranges all the way from complete subjection to their husbands to complete equality with them.[1] The subjection of women, like all slavery, has been enforced by legally established economic disadvantages; and upon the married woman these disadvantages, or some of them, are still binding in most communities. The law deprived her of the right to her own property and her own labour, and in return gave her a claim upon her husband for bare subsistence, which is the claim of a serf. Since woman's partial emergence from her subjection, and the consequent modification of the discriminations against her, laws which were logical and effective when her status was that of a chattel have been allowed to survive other laws which made them necessary. The result is a grotesque hodge-podge of illogical and contradictory provisions which involve injustice to both sexes, and

---

[1] The State of Wisconsin has made men and women equal before the law.

should be abolished by the simple expedient of making men and women equal in all respects before the law, and sweeping away all legal claims which they now exercise against one another by virtue of the marriage-bond.

This would mean, of course, that a woman might no longer legally claim support from her husband by virtue of her wifehood; nor should she in fairness be able to do so when all his claims to her property and services had been abolished. There is no reason why the disabilities which marriage imposes on women should be done away with and those which it imposes on men retained. To take such a course would be to turn the tables and place women in a position of privilege. The fact that women are still at considerable disadvantage in the industrial world might appear to justify such a position; but there is a better way of dealing with their economic handicaps than the way of penalizing husbands and demoralizing a large number of women by degrading marriage, for them, to the level of a means of livelihood, gained sometimes through virtual blackmail. Given complete equality of the sexes, so that prejudice may no longer avail itself of legal sanction for excluding women from the occupations in which they may elect to engage, the economic handicaps from which they may still suffer will be those resulting from the overcrowded condition of the general labour-market. The ultimate emancipation of woman, then, will depend not upon the abolition of the restrictions which have subjected her to man—that is but a step, though a necessary one—but upon *the abolition of all those restrictions of natural human rights that subject the mass of humanity to a privileged class.*

This phase of woman's problem is the main thesis of my book; and since it will come in for detailed consideration in subsequent chapters, I leave it for the present and proceed to discuss some probable results of sex-equality and the removal of legal claims which marriage now gives husband and wife against one another.

The wife would no longer be humiliated by the assumption that as a married woman she is the natural inferior of her husband, and entitled to society's protection against the extreme results of the disabilities that her status involves. If she became his housekeeper, she would do so by free choice, and not because her services were his legal property; and her resultant claim on his purse would be fixed by mutual arrangement rather than by laws allowing her the claims of a serf. The marriage, if it became an economic partnership, would be so by mutual consent and arrangement, and would thus no longer be a one-sided contract, legally defined, in which all the rights were on the side of the husband, but compensated in too many cases by unjust privileges on that of the wife. At the same time, the temptation to marry for economic security or ease would be lessened. This temptation besets both men and women, though not in the same degree, because men, through the economic advantage enjoyed by their sex, are oftener in a position of ease than women are. It is the temptation, arising out of man's natural desire to gratify his needs with the least possible exertion, to live by the means of others rather than by one's own labour. Its gratification through marriage would not be rendered impossible by the mere abolition of coercive laws governing the marriage relation; but at least its cruder manifestations, such as the frequent attempts of unscrupulous or demoralized women to use marriage for purposes of extortion, would no longer assail the nostrils of the public. Its reduction to a minimum must await the establishment of an economic order under which self-support will be easy and certain.

More general and binding, even, than the economic obligations that marriage entails are the personal claims that it creates. In so far as these claims are psychological—those of affection and habit, or attachment to children—their regulation and abrogation will always afford a problem which must be solved by the two persons concerned. There is at present a strong tendency to equalize the incidence of the laws whereby the State defines these relations and imposes them on married people. The old assumption of feminine inferiority in sexual rights is gradually yielding to a single standard for both sexes. So, also, the requirement that the wife shall in all matters subordinate her will and judgment to the will and judgment of her husband, tends to be modified by the new view of woman as a free agent rather than a mere adjunct to man. Qualifications for marriage and grounds for divorce tend to become the same for both sexes as the State is forced to relinquish its right to regard as offences in one sex actions which it does not recognize as offences in the other. It would appear, indeed, that the time is not far distant when the marriage-law, however humiliating its provisions may be, will bear equally on men and women.

But mere equalization of the law's incidence leaves untouched the previous question whether any third person—and the State assumes the rôle of a third person—has a legitimate right to define and regulate the personal relations of adult and presumably mature people. So long as the basic assumption goes unchallenged that the State may grant to man and woman lifelong monoply-rights in one another, or monopoly-rights which shall endure, despite the inclination of the persons concerned, during the State's pleasure, so long will complaints of harsh or unjust marriage or divorce laws prove the truth of Mill's dictum that "no enslaved class ever asked for complete liberty at once . . . those who are under any power of ancient origin, never begin by complaining of the power itself, but only of its oppressive exercise." Marriage under conditions arbitrarily fixed by an external agency is slavery; and if we allow the right of an external agency—be it State, family, or community—to place marriage in so degrading a position, we necessarily deny the freedom of the individual in this most intimate of relationships, and put ourselves in the position of petitioners for privilege when we sue for an improvement in the rules to which we have subjected ourselves.

When this fundamental fact is borne in mind, it becomes at once apparent that marriage will gain in dignity through the abolition of all legal sanction upon the personal claims that it involves. In a community which had renounced all claim to prescribe legally the nature of the marriage-bond, its duration, and the manner of its observance, there would be no washing of soiled domestic linen in the squalid publicity of courtrooms and newspaper-columns; no arbitration of noisy domestic differences by judges whose only qualification for the office is that they have had enough political influence to get themselves elected; none of the demoralizing consequences that the sense of proprietorship in one another has on the dispositions of married people. Marriage might still be publicly registered; it would no longer be publicly regulated. Its regulation would be left to the people whom it concerned, as it properly should be and safely could be; for as Mill remarked, "the modern conviction, the fruit of a thousand years experience, is that things in which the individual is the person directly interested, never go right but as they are left to his own discretion, and that any regulation of them by authority, save to protect the rights of others, is sure to be mischievous." The only way to protect married people against the bad faith which one may show toward the other, is to leave the door wide open for either of them to be quit of the union the minute it ceases to be satisfactory. If society for any reason sees fit to close the door to freedom, it sets union by law above the union by affection on which alone true marriage is based; and in so doing it is responsible for an amount of injustice, spiritual conflict, and suffering which no attempt at equitable regulation can ever compensate. Such attempts are in reality mere efforts to adjust the marriage-relation to the fundamental injustice of the marriage-law.

Perhaps the most serious objection to the union by law is that it is so often an effective barrier against the union by affection; for the union by law complicates marriage with a great many uses that are not properly germane to it; such as the custom of taking on one another's family and friends, and the setting up of a common menage where this most intimate and delicate of relationships is maintained in a trying semi-publicity under the critical and unwavering scrutiny of relatives and friends. The influence of the expected extends to the regulation of the menage and the division of labour. A lover would hardly, perhaps, require his mistress to darn his socks; but if she became his wife he would probably yield to the immemorial expectation that a married woman shall do her husband's mending. So, likewise, a woman may refuse to accept support from her lover so long as he is only her lover, and accept it as a matter of course when the union has been legalized. All conventional uses have a purely fortuitous and incidental connexion with marriage; yet they often fret it into failure. As Jane Littell remarked not long ago in the *Atlantic Monthly*, "being friends with someone to whom the law binds one is not so easy as it sounds." This is especially true where the law assumes a natural inferiority in one party to the contract, as it almost universally does.

I have not forgotten the children. One could hardly do so in an age when sentimentalism offers them as the final and unanswerable reason for continuing to tolerate the injustice involved in institutionalized marriage. But the very fact that it is the sentimentalist who thus defends established abuses is in itself enough to warrant considerable wariness in dealing with his arguments; for when the defenders of any cause have recourse to sentimentality, it is likely to be for want of solid ground under their feet, or in order to obscure a doubtful ulterior motive. Sentimentalism is a sugar coating on the pill of things as they are, which makes it easier for many people to swallow it than to contemplate a dose which is at once more salutary and more formidable, namely: things as they ought to be. When one hears the sentimentalist proclaiming the sacredness of marriage, one may agree with him; but at the same time one must wonder what kind of marriage he means; whether it is the ceremony performed by a minister or a magistrate, or the union which two people have made sacred through mutual respect, confidence and love. Such marriages as this last have sometimes been without benefit of clergy—Would these be as sacred to the sentimentalist as the marriage which has been sanctified only in law? Again, when one listens to the good old saws about the glory of motherhood, one may be interested to know the conditions under which it is proposed to call it glorious; and when domesticity is held up to admiration as woman's natural vocation, one wonders whether the sponsor of domesticity is willing to put his argument to the test by leaving her free to choose that vocation or not, as she will, or whether his praise is a mere preface to the demand that she be forced into this natural vocation by the method of denying her an alternative. So, likewise, when one hears the argument that marriage should be indissoluble for the sake of children, one cannot help wondering whether the protagonist is really such a firm friend of childhood, or whether his concern for the welfare of children is merely so much protective coloration for a constitutional and superstitious fear of change.

Children are really as helpless as women have always been held to be; and in their case the reason is not merely supposition. Woman was supposed to be undeveloped man. The child *is* undeveloped man or woman; and because of its lack of development it needs protection. To place it in the absolute power of its parents as its natural protectors and assume that its interests will invariably be well guarded, would be as cruel as was the assumption that a woman rendered legally and economically helpless and delivered over to a husband or other male guardian, was sure of humane treatment. No human being, man, woman, or child, may safely be entrusted to the power of another; for no human being may safely be trusted with absolute power. It is fair, therefore, that in the case of those whose physical or mental immaturity renders them comparatively helpless, there should be a watchful third person who from the vantage-point of a disinterested neutrality may detect and stop any infringement of their rights by their guardians, be they parents or other people. Here then, is a legitimate office for the community: to arbitrate, in the interest of justice, between children and their guardians.

But the community has a more direct and less disinterested concern in the welfare of children: every child is a potential power for good or ill; what its children become, that will the community become. It is knowledge of this that prompts the establishment of public schools and colleges, and all the manifold associational activities intended to promote the physical and spiritual welfare of children. It is back of the mothers' pension system, which is properly, as the Children's Bureau insists, a system of assistance for children. From all this activity it is only a step to the assumption by the community of entire responsibility for the upbringing and education of every child. This idea has some advocates; it is a perfectly logical corollary of the modern conception of the child's relation to the community. Yet it invites a wary and conditional acceptance. It is fair that the community should assume the burden of the child's support and education, particularly so long as the community sanctions an economic system which makes this burden too heavy for the great majority of parents, and a political system which may force male children to sacrifice their lives in war as soon as parents have completed the task of bringing them up. But the advisibility of accomplishing this purpose through the substitution of institutionalized care for parental care is more than a little doubtful; for to institutionalize means in great degree to mechanize. To establish such a system and make it obligatory, would be to remove many children from the custody of parents entirely unfitted to bring them up; but it would likewise involve the removal of many children from the custody of parents eminently well fitted for such a responsibility. It would imply an assumption that the people who might be engaged to substitute for parents would be better qualified for their task than the parents themselves; and such an assumption would be dangerous so long as the work of educators continues to be as little respected and as poorly paid as it now is. Moreover, so long as society remains organized in the exploiting State, the opportunity to corrupt young minds and turn out rubber-stamp patriots would be much greater than that which is now afforded by the public school system, whose influence intelligent parents are sometimes able to neutralize.

Perhaps the best argument against such a system is that it would not work. If experience teaches anything, it is that what the community undertakes to do is usually done badly. This is due in part to the temptation to corruption that such enterprises involve, but even more, perhaps, to the lack of personal interest on the part of those engaged in them. Those people who advocate bringing up children in institutions do not take into account the value of parental interest in the child; nor do they respect the parental affection which would cause many parents to suffer keenly if they were forced to part with their children. The family is by no means always the best milieu for young people; but before we seek to substitute a dubious institutionalism, it would be wise to ascertain whether the change is imperative. In a matter which touches, as this one does, the most profound human instincts, there is need to observe Lord Falkland's dictum that "where it is not necessary to change, it is necessary not to change." As I have shown in the preceding chapter, parents are at present under heavy economic handicaps in discharging their parental duties, handicaps which not only render those duties a heavy burden, but lengthen inordinately the period for which they must be undertaken. Until those handicaps are removed, it will not be fair to say that the family is a failure; and until they are removed, we may be certain that any other institution charged with the care of the young will be a failure, for it will be filled with people who are there less because of their understanding of children and their peculiar fitness to rear them, than because such work offers an avenue of escape from starvation.

These same considerations apply to the argument that the rearing of children should be institutionalized in order to emancipate women from the immemorial burden of "woman's work." There is a simpler way of dealing with this problem, a way which eliminates an element that dooms to failure any scheme of human affairs in which it is involved, namely: the element of coercion. To contend that all mothers should be forced to devote themselves exclusively to the rearing of children, or that they should be forcibly relieved of this responsibility, is to ignore the right of the individual to free choice in personal matters. There is no relation more intimately personal than that of parents to the child they have brought into the world; and there is therefore no relationship in which the community should be slower to interfere. This is a principle universally recognized: the community at present interferes only when the interest of the child, or that of the community in the child, is obviously suffering. The emancipation of women by no means necessitates the abandonment of this principle. It necessitates nothing more than a guarantee to women of free choice either to undertake themselves the actual work of caring for their children, or to delegate that work to others. There is nothing revolutionary about this: well-to-do parents have always exercised this choice. In mediaeval Europe people of the upper classes regularly sent their children to be brought up by other people, and took the children of other people into their own houses. In Renaissance

Italy the wealthy urban dwellers, almost as soon as their children were born, sent them out of the plague-infested cities to nurse with peasants. In modern times people who can afford it often place their children in boarding schools at an early age, and keep them at home only during vacations—when they do not place them in camps. Under a system of free economic opportunity all people, instead of a few, would have this alternative to rearing their children at home, for they would all be able to afford it. Even under the present economic order it would be possible if the system of children's assistance were extended to include every child, whether the parents were living or not. But under a system of free opportunity there would be greater certainty that the child would not suffer through separation from its parents; for the paid educator would be in his position because it interested him. If it did not, he would take advantage of the opportunity, freely open to him, to do something that did.

So long as responsibility for the care and support of children continues to be vested in the parents, so long, for the sake of the child, will it be the duty of society to insist that parents shall not neglect this responsibility. But when society had renounced all claim to regulate the affairs of married people, it would content itself with holding all parents, married or unmarried, jointly liable for the support and care of their children. If the parents were married, then the apportioning of this burden between them would be arranged by mutual agreement, and the community's only interest in the contract would be that of arbiter in case of a dispute between the parties, precisely as in case of other contracts. To assume that the community's interest in children justifies its claim to "preserve the home" by making marriage indissoluble or dissoluble only under humiliating conditions, is to confuse issues. The practice of perpetuating marriage merely for the sake of children defeats its own end; for it is, far from being good for children, likely to be injurious to them. It condemns them to be brought up in what Mr. Shaw has well called a little private hell. For the home, as other critics than Mr. Shaw have pointed out, is a proper place for children only when it provides harmonious conditions for their development; and harmony is not characteristic of homes where mutual love and confidence no longer exist between the parents. The demand that the freedom and happiness of parents shall be sacrificed to the so-called interest of the child is in reality a demand that injustice shall be done one person for the sake of another; and where this demand is effective it serves no end but that of frustration and discord, as might be expected. It is far better, as modern society is coming to realize, for the community to content itself with insisting upon the discharge of parental responsibility, without prescribing too minutely the conditions under which it shall be done.

It is not, perhaps, so much a concern for the preservation of the home that makes people afraid of divorce, as it is for other time-honoured concepts; such, for instance, as the idea that marriage is a sacrament, that it is made in heaven and is therefore indissoluble in this world. Curiously enough, this idea of the essential holiness and consequent indissolubility of the marriage-bond has coexisted in Christian society with the most cold-blooded practice of marrying for convenience, for money, for social prestige, for place and power, for everything that ignores or negates the spiritual element in sexual union. The marriage arranged for social or mercenary reasons by the families of the contracting parties, who might not even meet before the wedding-day, was as sacred as if it had been founded upon an intimate acquaintance and tender passion between them. Thus was utilitarianism invested with a spurious holiness. Small wonder that a mediaeval court of love denied the possibility of romantic attachment between husband and wife. The Church, to be sure, introduced the principle of free consent of the contracting parties; but so long as the subjection of women endured, there could be little more than a perfunctory regard for this principle. There can be no real freedom of consent when the alternative to an unwelcome marriage is the cloister or lifelong celibacy at the mercy of relatives whose wishes and interests one has defied, in a society where to be unmarried is, for a woman, to be nobody. A son, because of the greater independence that his sex gave him, might safely exercise some degree of choice in marrying. A daughter might safely exercise none. As women have become more independent, and their economic opportunities have increased, consent has become more closely related to inclination, and in many places, notably the United States, it is actually dependent upon inclination;[1] but

[1] In countries where the custom of dowry persists the parents are obviously in a position to exact a great degree of regard for their

Woman and Marriage

while women remain at an economic disadvantage it is hardly to be expected that the motives behind inclination and consent will always be entirely free from an ignoble self-interest.

So long as woman's economic and social welfare was bound up with marriage, indissoluble marriage undeniably offered her a certain kind of protection. It did not, as I have remarked, protect her from cruelty and infidelity on the part of her husband; but it generally assured her of a living and a respected position in society—that is, so long as she violated none of the conventional taboos against her sex. Even now the chivalrous man often feels that he must endure an unhappy marriage rather than cause his wife to incur the economic and social consequences of divorce. He generally feels that her chance of finding another husband to support her would be considerably worse than his of getting another wife to support; a feeling which, considering the relative desirability of supporting and being supported, will be justified so long as it is considered

wishes, more particularly where economic opportunity is no longer plentiful. In this country, where abundance of free land made the support of a family comparatively easy and secure, marriage early became a matter to be arranged by the contracting parties. In modern France, on the other hand, it is still largely a matter to be arranged between families.

tolerable for women to be an economic dead weight on the shoulders of men.

III

The sanctions of monogamic marriage have been enforced on women only. The Christian Church, after some indecision, finally decided that indissoluble monogamy was the only allowable form of marriage; and in theory it exacted from man and woman the same faithfulness to the marriage-vows. Practically, of course, it did no such thing. Being dominated by men, it eventually came to condone the sexual irregularities of men, if it did not sanction them; but sexual irregularity in the subject sex continued to be both theoretically and practically intolerable. Woman became the repository of morality in a society which regarded morality as chiefly a matter of sex. But since she was at the same time the means of satisfying those sexual needs which Christianity disparaged, she also bore the brunt of social displeasure at violation of the ascetic creed. Womankind, as I have already remarked, was divided into two classes: the virtuous wives and cloistered virgins who embodied Christian morals;

and those unfortunate social outcasts who sold their bodies to gratify un-Christian desires. The prostitute, the "companion" of the Greeks, who had been in the Greek world the only educated woman, the only woman who enjoyed comparative freedom, became in the Christian world a social outcast, reviled and persecuted, a convenient scapegoat for man's sins of the flesh, who atoned vicariously by her misery for his failure to live up to the Christian ideal of sexual purity. Nothing reflects more discredit upon the dominance of the male under Christianity than the fact that he took advantage of the economic helplessness which forced millions of women to sell their sex for a living, and then persecuted them outrageously because he had outrageously mistreated them. For prostitution, however much it may reflect upon the morality and, more especially, upon the taste, of men, has nothing whatever to do with the morality of women. It is, with women, a question of economics, purely and simply. The man who buys gratification of his sexual desire has at least an option in the matter; he will not starve if he abstains; but the woman who sells her body indiscriminately to any man who will buy, does so because her need to earn a living for herself or her family forces her to do violence to her natural selective sexual disposition.

This economic pressure has been strikingly illustrated in Central Europe since the war, where thousands of women of gentle breeding have been literally driven to the streets by the compelling scourge of want. The men upon whom these women in normal times would have depended for a living had been either killed or incapacitated in the war, or their power to earn had disappeared in the economic collapse which followed. When men, in a society so organized as to give them an economic advantage over women, can no longer earn enough to maintain their dependents even at the subsistence-level, the chance of women, for the most part untrained to breadwinning, to do so will be poor indeed. Under such circumstances the woman thrown on her own resources may, through some extraordinary stroke of luck, find a way to self-sufficiency through labour; but more often she is obliged, after her possessions have been disposed of, to take refuge from starvation by selling the only marketable commodity that is left her—her sex. Of course there is the alternative of starvation, which for herself she may choose; but if this choice would involve starvation for her children or other dependents she is likelier to choose prostitution, precisely as so many German and Austrian mothers and daughters have done. Mrs. O'Shaughnessy's little story of Vienna after the war, "Viennese Medley," depicts a situation which is not untypical. A middle-class Viennese family which had enjoyed a mediocre prosperity before the war, is suffering, with all that suffering city, from the nightmare of want that followed a savage peace. In the background, unspoken of, the only ray of hope across the bleakness of their extremity, moves the sister who sells her beauty to foreign officials and native, war-made millionaires. It is she who, when the young half-brother is struck by the dreaded plague of tuberculosis, sends him to the mountains and health. It is she who helps the sister-in-law to establish herself in trade, after the brilliant young surgeon, her brother, has come back a nervous ruin from the war. It is she who buries, with decent ceremony, the child of a sister whose husband, once a distinguished professor, is now able to do little more than starve with his numerous family. She even saves from want the young nobleman whom she loves, and his family as well. Not every woman who has sold herself in stricken Europe could command so high a price, but there is no doubt that many of them stood between their suffering families and death.

War releases all that is brutal in man, and places woman in a peculiarly helpless position; therefore it is a prolific immediate source of prostitution. But the ultimate and permanent source is the source of war itself, the economic exploitation of man by man. So long as society is organized to protect the exploiter, so long will peace be an incessant struggle—for more wealth with the privileged classes; for existence with the exploited masses—and war will be, as it has always been, merely a final explosion of the struggling forces. So long as human beings may starve in the midst of plenty, so long will woman be under temptation to sell the use of her body. She may prostitute herself because she has literally no other way to get a living; she may do so in order to eke out an insufficient wage; she may do so because prostitution seems to offer a relief from hopeless drudgery; she may do so because she has made what the world calls a misstep and is cut off thereby from respectability and the chance to earn a decent living; or she may prostitute herself legally, in marriage, as women have been forced to do from time immemorial. In every case there is one motive force, and that motive force is economic pressure, which bears hardest upon women because of the social, educational, and economic disadvantages from which they are forced to suffer in a world dominated by men. No amount of masculine chivalry has ever mitigated this evil, and no amount ever will; for chivalry is not compulsory, while prostitution is. No amount of exhortation, no amount of devoted labour on the part of reformers will touch it; for it is not a question of morality. No amount of persecution—of arrests, of man-handling, of night-courts, public insult, fine and imprisonment—will check it, for the necessity which prompts it is too imperious to be balked by the uncomprehending guardians of public decency. The peril of this necessity threatens all womankind; one turn of fortune's wheel may bring its stark aspect before the eyes of the most sheltered of women. It is the sheltered women, indeed, who are peculiarly in danger; those women whose preparation for the struggle to wrest a living from economic injustice has consisted in waiting for men to marry and support them. The parent who, in a world where celibacy and prostitution are on the increase, fails to give a girl child education or training which will enable her to get her living by her own efforts, forces her to take a dangerous risk; for the woman who is brought up in the expectation of getting her living by her sex may ultimately be driven to accept prostitution if she fails to find a husband, or, having found one, loses him.

There is only one remedy for prostitution, and that remedy is economic freedom—freedom to labour and to enjoy what one produces. When women have this freedom there will be no more prostitution; for no woman will get a living by doing violence to her deep-rooted selective instinct when opportunities are plentiful and a little labour will yield an ample living. There may still be women who are sexually promiscuous; but there is a vast gulf between promiscuity and prostitution: the sexually promiscuous woman may choose her men; the prostitute may not. It is the abysmal gulf between choice and necessity.

IV

Marriage, illegitimacy and prostitution are so closely related, as social problems, that it is impossible to draw firm lines of demarcation between

Woman and Marriage 143

them. The unlegalized union—which is betrayed by illegitimate birth—may be a marriage in all but law; the legalized marriage may be merely a respectable form of prostitution; prostitution may take the form of a more or less permanent union which may even assume the dignity of a true marriage. Illegitimacy, marriage, and prostitution do not exist independently; they exist in relation to one another and are often confused in people's minds—as when it is assumed that all mistresses are essentially harlots. They are the three faces of mankind's disastrous attempt to impose arbitrary regulation upon the unruly and terrifying force of sex; they form a triptych of which the central panel is institutionalized marriage and the other panels the two chief aspects of its failure. The title might appropriately be "The Martyrdom of Woman."

Experience has amply proved that as individualism progresses, it becomes increasingly difficult to impose upon people more than an appearance of conformity in sexual matters. Society can not really regulate anything so essentially personal and private in its nature as the sexual relation: it can only take revenge upon its natural result—and thereby encourage the prevention of that result by artificial means. For every unmarried mother who is persecuted by society, there are ten unmarried women who escape the social consequences of an unauthorized sexual relation. For every faithful husband there is another who deceives his wife with other women; nor are wedded wives by any means always faithful to their marriage vows. There are people who live together in the sexual uncleanness of loveless marriages; and there are those who live purely in extra-legal union. The sexual impulse is too variable and too imperious to be compressed into a formula.

Christian society, as I have remarked, early surrendered its uncompromising asceticism and settled down to an easy acceptance of the mere appearance of conventional sexual virtue—that is, so far as men were concerned. Women, as inferior and evil beings, who, incongruously enough, at the same time embodied Christian morality, must naturally be under the rigid surveillance of their male tutors, and no deviation from established rules might be allowed them. Thus worldly motives in marrying might be united with sacramental monogamy; for the man might avail himself of extra-marital union as a safety-valve for the emotional needs to which marriage gave no scope. The needs of the woman were not considered, save when savage punishment was visited upon their illicit satisfaction. Thus hypocrisy and deceit were tacitly encouraged, and the monogamic ideal was degraded; and countless generations lived a gigantic social lie which distorted and perverted their spiritual vision as only an accepted lie can distort and pervert it.

I do not mean by this that there have not been millions of really monogamous marriages. To intimate that the greater sexual freedom allowed men by law and custom has led all men into licence would be as stupid as to assume that repression and surveillance have kept all women chaste. But the institution of marriage, in Christian society, has represented compromise, and the fruit of compromise is insincerity—such insincerity, for example, as the Government of South Carolina shows when it forbids divorce, and fixes by law what proportion of his estate a man may leave to his concubine.

Any people which wishes to attain dignity and seriousness in its collective life must resolve to cast aside compromise and insincerity, and to look at all questions—even the vexed one of sex—squarely and honestly. The person who would do this has first some prepossessions to overcome: he must forget tradition long enough to appraise institutionalized marriage by its value to the human spirit; he must resolve for the time to regard men and women as equally human beings, entitled to be judged by the same standards, and not by different sets of traditional criteria; and he must put away fear of sex and fear of autonomy. If he can do these things, he may be able to look clear-eyed down the long vista of the centuries and realize the havoc that has been wrought in the souls of men and women by a sexual code and a system of marriage based on a double standard of spiritual values and of conduct. He may perceive how constant tutelage degrades the human spirit, and how much greater would be the sum of human joy if freedom were substituted for coercion and regulation—if men and women were without legal power to harass and bedevil one another simply because the State, through the marriage-bond, allows them humiliating rights in one another; if virginity and chastity were matters of self-respect and taste, instead of being matters of worldly self-interest to women and unconcern to men; if the relations between the sexes were based on equality and regulated only by affection and the desire to serve and give happiness.

Woman and Marriage

The modification which institutionalized marriage has been undergoing since the partial emergence of woman, its chief victim, have been in the direction of equality and freedom. The relative ease with which divorce may now be had marks a long step towards recognition of marriage as a personal rather than a social concern; and so does the tendency to abolish the legal disabilities resulting from the marriage-bond. Nothing augurs better for the elevation of marriage to a higher plane than the growing economic independence of women and the consequent improvement in the social position of the unmarried woman; for only when marriage is placed above all considerations of economic or social advantage will it be in a way to satisfy the highest demands of the human spirit.

But the emergence of women has had another significant effect, namely: an increase in frankness concerning extra-legal sexual relations, if not in their number. Of late there has been much public discussion of the wantonness of our modern youth; which, being interpreted, means the disposition of our girls to take the same liberty of indulgence in pre-nuptial sexual affairs that has always been countenanced in boys. This tendency is an entirely natural result of woman's increased freedom. The conditions of economic and social life have undergone revolutionary change in the past half-century; and codes of morals always yield before economic and social exigency, for this is imperious. It is for this reason, as Dr. A. Maude Royden has acutely observed, that women of the lower classes have always enjoyed a certain immunity from the taboos that reduced women of the middle and upper classes to virtual slavery. "If among the poor," says Dr. Royden, "these 'protections' have been dispensed with, it has not been because the poor have thought either better or worse of their women, but merely because they are too poor to dispense with their labour, and labour demands some small degree of freedom." Labour not only demands, it gives freedom. The woman who is economically independent need no longer observe rules based on male dominance; hence the new candour in woman's attitude towards the awe-inspiring fetich of sex.

If there is about this attitude an element of bravado, akin to that of the youth who thinks it clever and smart to carry a hip-pocket flask, it bears testimony, not to the dangers of freedom, but to the bankruptcy of conventional morality. The worst effect of tutelage is that it negates self-discipline, and therefore people suddenly released from it are almost bound to make fools of themselves. The women who are emerging from it, if they have not learned to substitute an enlightened self-interest for the morality of repression, are certainly in danger of carrying sexual freedom to dishevelling extremes, simply to demonstrate to themselves their emancipation from unjust conventions. There is no reason to expect that women, emerging from tutelage, will be wiser than men. One should expect the contrary. It is necessary to grow accustomed to freedom before one may walk in it sure-footedly. "Everything," says Goethe, "which frees our spirit without increasing our self-control, is deteriorating." This so-called wantonness, this silly bravado, simply shows that the new freedom is a step ahead of the self-discipline that will eventually take the place of surveillance and repression. It would not be so, perhaps, if girls and boys had ever been enlightened concerning the real sins of sex, and their true consequences. Women, in the past, have been taught to keep virgin or chaste for the sake of their reputations, of their families, of their chances in the marriage-market; they have been scared into chastity in the name of religion; but they have not been taught to be chaste for the sake of the spiritual value of chastity to themselves. Men, having been expected to "sow their wild oats, have been taught to sow them with a certain degree of circumspection. Girls have been intimidated by pictures of the social consequences of a misstep; boys have been warned of the physical danger involved in promiscuous sexual relations. This may not have been the invariable preparation of youth for the experiences of sex; but it has unquestionably been the usual one, and it is one of utter levity and indecency.

The real sins of sex are identical for men and women; and they differ from infractions of the conventional moral code in this respect among others: that they do not have to be found out in order to be punished. They carry their punishment in themselves, and that punishment is their deteriorative effect upon the human spirit. They are infractions of spiritual law; and there is this significant distinction to be observed between spiritual laws and the laws of men: that regulation plays no part in their administration. The law of freedom is the law of God, who does not attempt to regulate the human soul, but sets instinct there as a guide and leaves man free to choose whether he will follow the instinct which prompts obedience to spiritual law, or the desire which urges disregard of it. The extreme sophistication of the conventional attitude towards sex has dulled the voice of instinct for countless generations, with the inevitable result of much unnecessary suffering and irreparable spiritual loss.

A healthy instinct warns against lightness in sexual relationships; and with reason, for the impulse of sex is one of the strongest motive forces in human development and human action. It touches the obscurest depths of the soul; it affects profoundly the functions of the mind and the imagination—can not, indeed, be dissociated from them. The fact that it is also strongly physical leads to misunderstanding and disregard of its relation to the mind and spirit; a misunderstanding and disregard which are immensely aggravated in a society where woman, because of her inferior position, may be used for the gratification of physical desire, with no consideration of her own desires or her spiritual claims. Prostitution, for example, has exerted a most deleterious influence on the attitude of men toward sex and toward women. But degradation of the sex-impulse is inevitably punished. The sheerly physical indulgence to which it leads produces a coarsening of spiritual fibre, an incapacity for appreciation of spiritual values. Moreover, it produces a cleavage between passion and affection which renders impossible the highest and most beautiful form of the sexual relation, the relation in which passion and affection are fused in a love which offers complete understanding and fulfilment. It is to this fusion (and not to monogamy, which, Spencer thought, developed love) that we owe "the many and keen pleasures derived from music, poetry, fiction, the drama, etc., all of them having for their predominant theme the passion of love." True monogamy, the product of this highest love, is not a regulation to be observed; it is an ideal to be attained, and it will not be attained by the person who fails to recognize and to respect the spiritual aspects of the sexual relation.

Nor will it be attained by the person who mistakes excitement for love, and who flits from one temporary attachment to another, thinking always to find the beautiful in the new. Such promiscuous philandering not only precludes depth of affection and thus renders constancy impossible; it also blunts perception. Its effect was never better expressed than by Burns, who was one of its unhappy victims.

> I waive the quantum o' the sin,
> The hazard of concealin',
> But och! it hardens a' within,
> And petrifies the feelin'.

This is the penalty of levity in human relations: that it *petrifies feeling*. One pays the price in spiritual deterioration. There is probably no more striking testimony to this than the first part of Goethe's "Faust." Consider what we know of the nature of Goethe's relations with women; and then consider the spiritual insensitivity, the failure to perceive and draw upon the inexhaustible spiritual treasures that life holds in store, that are implied in his failure to devise for Faust, brought back from the brink of the grave at cost of his immortal soul, any more animating employment for his new-found youth than a low intrigue with an ignorant peasant girl.

I will pass by the contention that men are by nature polygamous and women monogamous; for it rests on evidence created by a dual standard of conduct for the sexes. Certain women of independent spirit are at present rather conspicuously engaged in proving themselves not merely polygamous but promiscuous; and a great many men have always proved themselves to be monogamous. Probably human beings vary in respect of these tendencies as of others. All people, perhaps, can not attain the highest plane in love, either for want of capacity or of opportunity; nor can all people conform to a single mode of conduct. But all people can attain sincerity in sexual relations, and at least a certain degree of self-knowledge. Sincerity, self-knowledge, respect for oneself and for other people; these are essential to a genuine ethic of sex; and they are uncontemplated by the sanctions of conventional morality. Yet the person who violates this ethic sins against his own spirit, which is to sin against the Holy Ghost, and on the spiritual plane he will be punished.

An increase in extra-legal relationships does not of itself imply spiritual retrogression. It might imply instead one of two things, or both, namely: an increase in the economic obstacles to legal marriage; or a growing disinclination to admit an affair so personal as the sex-relation to sanction and regulation by people whom it did not concern. If men and women were economically equal and independent, the number of marriages might increase enormously; on the other hand, institutionalized marriage might be superseded by marriage without legal sanction, which before the birth of children might not be even known or recognized as marriage.[1] Free people would probably want less of official interference in their personal affairs, rather than more. But for those who wanted to avoid the terrors of autonomy there would still be marriage; and for those who wanted to walk in the strait and ennobling way of freedom, there would be the right to love without official permission, and to bring forth children unashamed. Those who wished to sell themselves would be free to do so if they could find buyers; but no one would be forced to live by violating the law of love which is the law of life. Freedom implies the right to live badly, but it also implies the right to live nobly and beautifully; and for one who has faith in the essential goodness of the human spirit, in the natural aspiration towards

---

[1] Several feminists have already, indeed, urged public sanction of extra-legal sexual relations, and C. Gasquoine Hartley, with a genuinely Teutonic passion for order, has even advocated their regulation by the State. This is probably impossible, for people who choose such relationships usually do so to escape regulation.

perfection which flowers with touching beauty even in the bleak soil of that hardship, degradation and crime to which injustice condemns the mass of humanity—for one who has this faith in the human spirit, there can be no question what its ultimate choice would be.

CHAPTER V

THE ECONOMIC POSITION OF WOMEN

I

It is to the industrial revolution more than anything else, perhaps, that women owe such freedom as they now enjoy; yet if proof were wanting of the distance they have still to cover in order to attain, not freedom, but mere equality with men, their position in the industrial world would amply supply it. Men in industry suffer from injustices and hardships due to the overcrowding of the labour-market. Women suffer from these same injustices and hardships; and they have an additional handicap in their sex. The world of work, embracing industry, business, the professions, is primarily a man's world. Women are admitted, but not yet on an equal footing. Their opportunities for employment are restricted, sometimes by law, but more often by lack of training; and their remuneration as wage-earners and salaried workers is generally less than that of men. They have to contend with traditional notions of what occupations are fitting for their sex; with the jealousy of male workers; with the prejudices of employers; and finally with their own inertia and their own addiction to traditional concepts. All these difficulties are immensely aggravated by the keenness of the competition for work. If the opportunity to work were, as it should be, an unimpeded right instead of a privilege doled out by an employer, these handicaps of women would be easily overridden by the demand for their labour. I shall discuss this point more fully later on. It is sufficient here to note that when the war created a temporary shortage of labour, women were not only employed in, but were urged in the name of patriotism to enter, occupations in which until then only men had been employed. The effect of this temporary shortage on their industrial opportunities affords a hint of what their position would be if the glutting of the labour-market were permanently relieved. A shortage of labour means opportunity for the worker, male or female.

Women have always been industrial workers. Otis T. Mason even went so far as to declare that "All the peaceful arts of today were once woman's peculiar province. Along the lines of industrialism she was pioneer, inventor, author, originator."

This view is in rather striking contrast with the contemptuous derogation which has been for a long time current in European civilization, and has found expression in such cutting remarks as that of Proudhon, that woman "could not even invent her own distaff." It is no doubt a fairer view, although it is probably somewhat exaggerated. There is certainly no valid reason to suppose that sex is a barrier to the invention and improvement of industrial processes. Be this as it may, it is undeniable that women have always been producers. Among some primitive tribes, indeed, they are the only industrialists, the men occupying themselves with war and the chase or, among maritime peoples, with fishing. The modern invasion of the industrial field by women does not, then, represent an attempt to do something that women have never done before. It does represent an attempt to adapt themselves to the new conditions created by the industrial revolution.

The range of their opportunities has been considerably restricted by prejudices arising from the traditional sexual division of labour in European society. "In the developed barbarism of Europe, only a few simple household industries were on the whole left to women."[1] It was natural, then, when women followed industry into the larger field of machine-production, that it should be assumed that the industries in which they might fittingly engage would be those most nearly akin to the occupations which European society has regarded as peculiarly feminine. Before the World War, according to the Women's Bureau, "over seventy-five per cent of all women engaged in manufacture were concentrated in the textile and garment-making industries"; and we have the same authority for the statement that "except for certain branches of food-manufacture—such as flour making . . . women constitute from a third to two-thirds of the working forces in the industries concerned with the business of clothing and feeding both the fighting and the civilian population." The new opportunities opened up by the exigency of the war-period widened considerably the scope of women's activity; they were employed in machine-shops and tool-rooms, in steel- and rolling-mills, in instrument-factories, in factories manufacturing sewing machines and typewriters, in utensil-factories, in plants working in rubber and leather, in wood-working industries.

[1] Ellis: Man and Woman. 5th ed. p. 14.

Economic Position of Women 161

In some of these industries women continue to be employed. In others they were discharged to make room for men when the emergency was over. But even where they continue to be employed their opportunities for training are not equal to those of men. The Women's Bureau in 1922 issued a valuable bulletin on "Industrial Opportunities and Training for Women and Girls." According to this bulletin, the war-experience of women in new employments made it apparent that the most promising future for craftswomen in these fields lies in (a) machine-shops where light parts are made, (b) wood-product factories where assembling and finishing are important processes, (c) optical- and instrument-factories, (d) sheet-metal shops. The survey made by the Bureau to discover how many of the country's industrial training schools were fitting women for these trades disclosed the fact that in nine States where women, because of industrial conditions, are most in need of training for machine-shop, sheet-metal, furniture, or optical work, they are either excluded by public vocational schools from the courses in such works, or they are not encouraged, as men are, to enter those courses. In Ohio, for example, women were enrolled in only five of the fifty-three public vocational schools reporting, and in these five schools they were taught dressmaking, costume-design, dress-pattern making, embroidery, power-machine sewing, and pottery making. Men on the other hand, received instruction in the following courses which women needed: machine-shop practice, tool-making, shop mathematics, mechanical drafting, blue-print reading, metallurgy, pattern-making, sheet-metal work, welding, auto-mechanics and repair, motor-cycle mechanics, gas engineering, cabinet-making and woodworking. Women were not debarred by rule or law from entering these courses, but they were not encouraged to do so. The courses, as one superintendent wrote, were "designed for men." The situation in Ohio is more or less the same as that in the other eight States. Women are either not admitted to vocational courses designed to prepare workers for the industries cited, or they are not encouraged to enroll. Yet, as the Bureau points out, these institutions are operated at the expense of the taxpayers, women as well as men, and their equipment should be used to serve women as well as men. "It is obvious," says the Bureau, "that the public vocational school authorities, with few exceptions,

Economic Position of Women

think of trade for women only in terms of dressmaking and millinery, and are as yet quite oblivious to the fact that these trades, except in certain clothing centers, are not the big employers of woman labour, nor are they always the best trades at which to earn a livelihood. It is the semi-public school that is beginning first to recognize the new position which woman occupies in industry as a result of the war and is opening to her its doors and guiding her into courses leading to efficiency in the new occupations."

This blindness of the school authorities to the vocational needs of women goes to prove how strong is the force of traditional prejudices. The making of clothing has been largely in the hands of women for so long that even in cities where the only industries employing women are mechanical or woodworking, the public schools offer them courses in sewing and millinery. Prepossession does not yield all at once to established fact. If women can make a permanent place for themselves in their new occupations, public officials will eventually come to associate them with these occupations and follow the lead of the semi-public schools in fitting girls to engage in them on an equal footing with boys.

But it will take time; and meanwhile women will continue to be at a disadvantage in entering these occupations. So will they be at a disadvantage in entering any occupation where they have not before been employed, or where they are employed only in insignificant numbers, so long as prejudice or conservatism continues to debar them, and the necessary training is not as freely available to them as it is to men.

Above all, so long as their industrial status continues to be, as the Women's Bureau expresses it, "subsidiary to their home status," they can never be on a really secure footing in the industrial world. While employers assume that all male workers have families to support and that all female workers are in industry rather through choice than necessity and may, in periods when work is slack, fall back on the support of male relatives, so long will women be the first workers to suffer from any slowing down of industry. This was strikingly illustrated during the period of unemployment which succeeded the intense industrial activity made necessary by the war, when women were discharged in great numbers to make room for men, and much resentment was voiced against their retention in places which might be filled by men. "Back to the home," says the Women's Bureau, "was a slogan all too easily and indiscriminately flung at the wage-earning woman by those who had little conception of the causes which forced her into wage-earning pursuits." In periods of industrial depression it appears to be the regular practice to lay off the married women workers first, then the single women, and the men last.

How unjust to the woman worker, and how little justified by actual facts, is this survival of the idea that woman's place is the home, has been shown through investigations undertaken by the Women's Bureau and other agencies. The results of these investigations, published in Bulletin No. 30 of the Women's Bureau, show that the woman in industry is not merely working for pin-money, as thoughtless people assume, but that she is more often not only supporting herself on her inadequate wage, but contributing materially to the support of dependents. "Contributing all earnings to the family fund," says the Bureau, "is a very general practice among wage-earning women." This of course means, as the Bureau remarks, that however much or little her contribution may mean to the family, for the woman herself it means a surrender of economic independence. The contrast between single men and single women in this respect is significant. In an investigation conducted among workers in the shoe-making industry of Manchester, New Hampshire, the Bureau found that "comparing single men and women, the women contributed (to the family income) more extensively, both actually and relatively." The percentage of earnings contributed by sons and daughters is particularly interesting. The Bureau found that "in the families with per capita earnings of less than $500, 49.3 per cent of the sons and 71.6 per cent of the daughters contributed all their earnings, while in families with per capita earnings of $500 or more, 36.8 per cent of the sons and 53.4 per cent of the daughters contributed all earnings." When one remembers that the wage paid to women was so much lower than that paid to men that the Bureau pronounced them to be scarcely comparable, the fact that "the daughters contributed a somewhat larger proportion of the family earnings than did the sons" takes on added significance. The sons contributed almost as much in actual money as the daughters, but out of their higher wages they retained something for themselves, "thus assuring themselves of a degree of independence and an opportunity to strike out for themselves which is denied the daughters."

It is evident, then, that women, even in the "emancipation" of the industrial world, are continuing their immemorial self-sacrifice to the family, and that it is not the married woman alone, but the single woman as well, who makes this sacrifice. The conditions of the sacrifice have changed with the changes in industry, but the sacrifice continues. The productive labour of women appears to be quite as indispensable to their families as it was in the days when they spun and wove and sewed and baked at home. This being the case, there is obviously no other ground than prejudice for the assumption that men, as the natural providers, should have preference in the labour-market. According to the census of 1920, thirty-five per cent of the men in the country are single; therefore it is fair to assume that thirty-five per cent of the men in industry are single. Two-thirds of the women in industry are single, but the available figures show that a much larger percentage of these women than of single men are contributing all or most of their earnings to their families, while married women workers are contributing all of their earnings. In view of these figures, there is patent injustice in the assumption that all men and no women have dependents to support.

So is there injustice in the assumption that women are naturally at least partly dependent on male workers, and therefore may fairly be forced to accept a smaller wage than men. This assumption is not only grossly unfair to the woman worker, but it does not tally with fact. A fine example of the kind of defence for the practice of sweating women workers that can be based on this assumption is quoted by the Women's Bureau from an unnamed commercial magazine. "Eighty-six per cent of women workers," runs this masterpiece of sophistry, "live at home or with relatives. [So, in all likelihood, do eighty-six per cent of male workers.] It is immaterial in these cases whether the earnings of each measure up to the cost of living scheduled for a single woman living alone, so that the theory of the need of a sufficient wage to support a single woman living alone does not apply to eighty-six per cent of the entire population [*sic*]." This quotation, says the Bureau, is typical of the attitude of the employer who pays his women employees less than a living wage on the plea that they live at home and therefore have few expenses. It is equally remarkable in its ruthless disregard of the just claim of the woman worker to the same share in the product of her toil that the male worker is allowed; and in its disregard of the fact that so long as eighty-six per cent of women workers are forced to accept a starvation-wage because they live at home, the other fourteen per cent who do not live at home will be forced by the pressure of competition to accept the same starvation-wage. The question how this fourteen per cent will eke out a living—whether through overwork, begging or prostitution—does not of course concern the employer; for it is one of the striking differences between chattel-slavery and wage-slavery that the owner of the wage-slave is under no obligation to keep his workers from starving. That is, presumably, their own lookout.

If employers are not given to concerning themselves with this question, however, communities are. Thirteen States have enacted laws fixing a minimum wage for women, three have fixed minimum wages in specified occupations, one has fixed a minimum wage which its industrial welfare commission has power to change, and nine have created boards or commissions with power to fix minimum wage-rates. It may be noted that in those States where the rate is fixed by law, it has not responded to the rising cost of living. In Utah and Arkansas, for example, the minimum wage for an experienced woman is $7.50 a week. There is constant effort by interested individuals and organizations to get similar laws enacted in other States, in spite of the fact that in 1923 the Supreme Court of the United States declared unconstitutional the minimum wage-law of the District of Columbia. Such efforts, of course, are in reality efforts to secure class-legislation, as are all attempts to secure special enactments designed to benefit or protect women.

Of such enactments there is an ever increasing number. So rapidly do they increase, indeed, that women may be said to be in a fair way to exchange the tyranny of men for that of organized uplift. They are sponsored by those well-meaning individuals who deplore social injustice enough to yearn to mitigate its evil results, but do not understand it well enough to attack its causes; by women's organizations whose intelligence is hardly commensurate with their zeal to uplift their sex; and by men's labour-organizations which are quite frankly in favour of any legislation that will lessen the chances of women to compete with men in the labour-market.[1] Given the combined suasion of these forces, and the inveterate sentimentalism which makes it hard for legislators to resist any plea on behalf of "the women and children," almost anything in the way of rash and ill-considered legislation is possible, and even probable. There is on the statute-books of the various States an imposing array of laws designed to "protect" women workers. There are only four States which do not in some way limit the hours of work for women; there are eleven which limit the number of successive days that they may work; fourteen have fixed the amount of time that shall be allowed them

[1] Katharine Anthony found the workmen of Germany frankly in favour of any "protective" legislation that would hamper German working women ("Feminism in Germany and Scandinavia"); and the Woman's Party has met with the same attitude among unions in this country. Among the resolutions passed at the twenty-fifth convention of the International Moulders' Union of North America was the following: "*Resolved*, that the decision of this convention be the restriction of the further employment of child and woman labour in union core rooms and foundries, and eventually the elimination of such labour in all foundries by the example set by union foundries in the uplifting of humanity. . . . *Resolved*, that the incoming officers be directed to, either by themselvs or in co-operation with others in the labour movement, give their best thought and effort in opposing the employment of female and child labour in jobs recognized as men's employment."

for their midday meal; twelve have ruled that a woman may work only a given number of hours without a rest-period. Sixteen States prohibit night-work in certain industries or occupations; two limit her hours of night-work to eight. There is also a tendency to extend to women special protection against the hazards of industry. In seventeen States the employment of women in mines is prohibited. Two States prohibit their employment in any industry using abrasives. In four States they are not allowed to oil moving machinery. Three regulate their employment in core-making; and four regulate the amount of the weight that they may be required to lift—the maximum ranging, oddly enough, from fifteen pounds in Ohio and Pennsylvania to seventy-four pounds in Massachusetts. In addition to those regulations which prohibit women from working in certain occupations or under certain conditions, "each State," says the Women's Bureau, "has many laws and rulings which prescribe the conditions under which women should work, covering such matters as the lifting of weights, provision of seats, and proper provision for sanitation and comfort." In six States, industrial commissions have power to make regulations

Economic Position of Women 173

for the health and welfare of workers. In three, the commissions have power to make regulations for women and minors only, and in one, for women, minors, learners, and apprentices.

Perhaps the most striking thing about all these multiform regulations governing the employment of women is the amount of misplaced zeal that they denote. "In most cases," says the Women's Bureau, "the laws which prohibit their employment have little bearing on the real hazards to which they are exposed. . . . Prohibiting the employment of women on certain dusty processes does not solve the problem of any industrial disease in a community. Men are also liable to contract pulmonary diseases from exposure to dusts. . . . It is very possible that under the guise of 'protection' women may be shut out from occupations which are really less harmful to them than much of the tedious, heavy work both in the home and in the factory which has long been considered their special province. *Safe standards of work for women must come to be safe standards for men also if women are to have an equal chance in industry.*" The italics are mine. It is worth mentioning here that only two States prohibit the employment of women in the lead-industry, which so far is the only one that has been proved more harmful to women than to men. The mass of legislation and regulation designed to protect women from the fatigues and hazards of industry would seem, then, to have been animated more by chivalry than by scientific knowledge; and while chivalry may be all very well in its place, it can hardly be expected to solve the industrial problem of women.

In connexion with so-called welfare-legislation, it is interesting to observe that women and children are customarily grouped together as classes requiring protection; and that various laws affecting their position in industry have been sanctioned by the courts as being for the good of the race and therefore not to be regarded as class-legislation. Such decisions certainly would appear to be reasonable in so far as they apply to children, who are the rising generation of men and women, and should be protected during their immaturity. But they can be held valid as they affect women only if woman is regarded as primarily a reproductive function. This view, apparently, is held by most legislators, courts, and uplifters; and they have an unquestionable right to hold it. Whether, however, they are

Economic Position of Women 175

just in attempting to add to the burdens of the working woman by imposing it upon her in the form of rules that restrict her opportunities, is another question. One thing is certain: if discriminative laws and customs are to continue to restrict the opportunities of women and hamper them in their undertakings, it makes little difference for whose benefit those laws and customs are supposed to operate, whether for the benefit of men, of the home, of the race, or of women themselves; their effect on the mind of woman and her opportunities, will be the same. While society discriminates against her sex, for whatever reason, she can not be free as an individual.

Should nothing, then, be done to protect women from the disabilities and hazards to which they are subject in the industrial world? Better nothing, perhaps, than protection which creates new disabilities. Laws which fix fewer hours of work for women than for men may result in shortening men's hours also in factories where many women are employed; but they may result in the substitution of men—or children—for women in factories where but few have been employed. Laws prohibiting night-work may reduce the chances of women to get much-needed employment, and may sometimes shut them out of work which would offer higher returns on their labour than anything they might get to do during the day—as, for example, night-work in restaurants, where the generous tips of after-theatre patrons add considerably to the earnings of waiters. Moreover, it is hard to see on what ground night-work could be held to be more harmful for women than for men. Minimum-wage laws may fix a legal limit to the greed of employers, but they can not prevent the underpayment of women workers, for they are based on theoretical notions of a living wage, and have no relation to the actual value of the individual's labour. Where they are fixed by law, as I have remarked, a rise in the cost of living may render them ineffectual. As for those laws which undertake to protect women against the hazards of industry, they have usually, as the Women's Bureau has shown, very little relation to the hazards to which women are actually exposed; but they constitute a real barrier to industrial opportunity. On the whole, the vast and unwieldy array of laws and rules designed either to protect the woman worker, or to safeguard the future of the race at her expense, are a pretty lame result of a great deal of humanitarian sound and fury. *Parturiunt montes*.

It is quite natural that the result should be lame; for these protections and safeguards represent so many attempts to mind some one else's business; and the great difficulty about minding some one else's business is that however good one's intentions may be, one can never really know just where that some one's real interests lie, or perfectly understand the circumstances under which he may be most advantageously placed in the way to advance them, for the circumstances are too intimately bound up with his peculiar temperament and situation. As Mill has remarked in a passage which I have already quoted, the world has learned by long experience that affairs in which the individual is the person directly interested go right only when they are left to his own discretion, and that any interference by authority, save to protect the rights of others, is mischievous. The tendency of modern welfare-legislation is to make a complete sacrifice of individual rights not to the rights but to the hypothetical interests of others; and for every individual who happens to benefit by the sacrifice, there is another who suffers by it. If it is hard to regulate one human being for his own good, it is impossible to regulate people *en masse* for their own good; for there is no way of making a general rule affect all individuals in the same way, since no two individuals are to be found who are of precisely the same temperament and in precisely the same situation.

There is in all this bungling effort to ameliorate the ills of working women and to safeguard through them the future of the race, a tacit recognition of economic injustice and a strange incuriousness about its causes. One would naturally expect that the conditions which move people to seek protective legislation would move them to question the nature of an economic system which permits such rapacity that any class of employees requires to be protected from it. Surely the forces of righteousness must know that there are reasons for the existence of the conditions which move them to pity and alarm; yet they seem quite willing to go on indefinitely battling against the conditions, and winning with great effort legislative victories which are constantly being rendered ineffectual through lax administration of laws, through the reluctance of employees to jeopardize their positions by testifying against employers, or through unforeseen changes in economic conditions. During all this waste of time and effort, this building and crumbling and rebuilding of protective walls around the labourer, the causes of economic injustice continue their incessant operation, producing continuously a new crop of effects which are like so many windmills inviting attack by the Don Quixotes of reform.

Let us consider the effects of economic injustice on women, side by side with the reformer's work upon those effects. Women in industry suffer, as I have shown, the injustice of inequality with men as regards wages, opportunities, training, and tenure of employment. The reformer attacks the problem of wages, and secures minimum-wage laws based on some one's theory of what constitutes a living wage. No allowance is made for dependents because women, theoretically, have none. The amount allowed may from the first be inadequate, even for one person, or it may be rendered inadequate by a rise in the cost of living. In either case, it is purely arbitrary, and bears no relation whatever to the value of the worker's services. Still, such legislation might be better than nothing if there were nothing better to be done. The reformer is less zealous in his attempt to provide women with opportunities; his showing in this field is less impressive than in that of wages. Still, he has done something. If he has not been entirely responsible for the opening to women of many positions in government service, he has at least greatly assisted in securing them these opportunities. Farther than this, it must be admitted, it is difficult for him to go. He might, indeed, exert himself to see that women are provided by one means or another with equal opportunities to get training, but he can do little to affect the policies of private employers of labour, who can hardly be dictated to concerning whom they shall hire and whom they shall retain. Nor can he prevent employers from laying off women workers first when there is a slowing down in production. In three, then, out of four of the disadvantages which bear more heavily on women in industry than on men, the reformer, with all his excellent intentions, is unable to be very helpful; while in his zeal to safeguard the race, whose future appears to him to depend entirely on the health of the female sex, he has multiplied their disadvantages in the manner I have already described, without, however, having made any noteworthy advance toward the accomplishment of his purpose.

Now, had he chosen to inquire into the causes of the artificial disabilities by which women workers are handicapped, he might have discovered that these and the industrial hazards which cause him such grave concern may be traced to the same fundamental source; and that the just and only effective way of removing these disabilities and hazards is to eradicate the source. Women in industry are the victims of traditional prejudices: I have shown what those prejudices are—the idea that woman's place is the home, that women workers have no dependents, that they work for pin-money and therefore do not need a living wage, that upon them alone depends the future health of the race. But as I remarked at the beginning of this chapter, these prejudices could not be turned to the disadvantage of the woman worker if it were not for the overcrowding of the labour-market. So long as there are more people looking for work than there are jobs to be had, the advantage in fixing terms and conditions of labour is on the side of the employer. If men are obliged by their need to put up with underpayment, women will be forced to accept an even worse rate; if the tenure of men is uncertain, that of women will be even more so. If the conditions of industry are hazardous, the alternative of starvation will force the workers to risk injury or death unless the employer be required by law to maintain the proper safeguards. Suppose, however, that labour were scarce, that for every worker looking for employment there were a dozen employers looking for workers. Under such circumstances, the employer would be glad enough to hire the worker who could fill his particular requirements, without regard to sex, as employers did during the war when labour was scarce; and he would pay the worker a wage determined not by theory or prejudice, but by the amount of competition for the worker's services. If the employment he offered were hazardous, he would be obliged to maintain proper safeguards in order to retain his employees, and in addition would probably be forced to pay them a higher wage than they could earn in some safer employment. If he did not do these things, his workers would simply leave him for more satisfactory positions. Nor would he be able to overwork his employees, for if he attempted to do so, some rival employer would outbid him for their services by offering better hours and easier conditions of labour. Thus the peculiar disabilities of women workers would disappear with the disabilities of labourers in general, and not a stroke of legislation would be required to make industry both safe and profitable for the woman worker.

This condition is not unnatural or impossible. It is the present condition of chronic unemployent, of expensive and ineffectual "welfare" legislation, of wasteful and futile struggles between organized capital and organized labour—it is this condition that is entirely unnatural. I have mentioned its cause in Chapter III, and I shall discuss it further in my next chapter. Upon its removal, and not upon regulations which hamper the woman worker and reduce her to the status of a function, the future of the race depends. The ancestors of coming generations are men as well as women, and posterity will derive its heritage of health from its ancestors of both sexes. Its prospect of health will not be improved by legislation calculated to safeguard the health of women workers, so long as the children they bear continue to be exposed to an involuntary poverty which breeds ignorance, imbecility, disease and crime. The happiness as well as the health of future generations will depend in great measure upon the extent to which both men and women can release themselves from the deteriorating conditions of economic exploitation.

II

It is in business and in professional pursuits that the occupational progress of women, and their emancipation from traditional prejudices, are most marked. Although in the lower ranks of labour in these pursuits there is a mass of women who, impelled by necessity, work for low wages at mechanical tasks which offer no chance of advancement, there is, nearer the top, a large group of women who have been more fortunate in worldly position and education, and who are spurred as much either by interest in their work or a desire to be self-supporting, as by actual need to earn; who share, in other words, the attitude that leads young men to strike out for themselves even though their fathers may be able to support them. It is the woman animated by these motives who is doing most for the advancement of her sex; for it is she, and not the woman who works through necessity, who really challenges the traditional prejudices concerning the proper place of women. The woman labourer proves the *need* of women to earn; the business woman or professional woman who works because she wants to work, is establishing the *right* of women to earn. More than this, as she makes her way into one after another of the occupations that have been held to belong to men by prescriptive right, she is establishing her claim, as a human being, to choose her work from the whole wide field of human activity. It is owing to the attitude towards life adopted by such women, to their preference of independence and action over the dependence and passivity in vogue not so many years ago, that it is coming to be quite the expected thing that young women of the well-to-do classes shall set out to earn their living, as young men do, instead of stopping under the parental roof, with a watchful eye out for men who will marry and support them. Need I remark that nothing is more likely than this new attitude to bring about the substitution of the "union by affection" for the union by interest? The woman who is economically independent is under much less temptation to marry from economic motives than the woman for whom marriage represents the only prospect of security.

There is still a goodly number of prejudices and discriminations to be overcome before women in business and the professions shall stand on an equal footing with men as regards opportunity and remuneration. Except where she is in business for herself, the woman in these pursuits must generally be content with a lower rate of pay than men; and if observation may be taken to count for anything, she is expected to work somewhat harder for what she gets—less loafing on the job is tolerated in her than in the male employee. She is also more likely to find herself pocketed; that is to say, in a position from which, because of her sex, there is no possibility of further advance because the higher positions are reserved for men. It is so universally the rule that women must content themselves with reaching the lower rungs of the occupational ladder, that the instances where they manage to attain to places of responsibility and authority are still rare enough to be found worthy of remark in the press. The same thing is true of political positions; women are not yet represented in politics in anything like a just proportion to their numbers, nor are they often able to get themselves either elected or appointed to responsible positions. None the less, considering the comparatively short time since their emergence into the business world and the world of public affairs, they are already making an excellent showing.

The world of business and the professions, like the world of industry, has its occupations which are considered peculiarly suitable for women. Strictly subordinate positions are thought to suit them very well; hence there is quite an army of women stenographers, bookkeepers, clerks and secretaries to be found in the business section of any modern city. The personnel of the nursing profession is made up almost exclusively of women; and the work of teaching in our public schools, especially where it is most conspicuously underpaid, is largely in their hands. There is, to be sure, an impression current among members of school boards that marriage disqualifies a woman for the teaching profession; but the single woman is fairly secure in her position, possibly because it does not pay well enough to be very attractive to men. Occupations connected with the arts are also held, in this country, to be particularly well adapted for women, although it must be noted that the prejudice of male musicians is effective enough to exclude them from the personnel of our important orchestras. It is in the creative arts that their work is most welcomed; more especially in the field of literature; and this may seem strange, in view of the fact that so many eminent authorities believe that their sex renders them incapable of attaining any significance in creative work. It is, I apprehend, rather to the low opinion in which aesthetic pursuits are held in this country than to a high opinion of female ability, that this peculiar condition must be ascribed.

But if certain occupations are considered peculiarly appropriate for women, there is none the less a great deal of prejudice against them in others. The idea that woman's place is the home has no more disappeared from the world of business and the professions than it has disappeared from the world of industry, even though it is the business woman and the professional woman who are doing most to dislodge it. And here it may be well to remark a fact that has already been noted, with some pointed comment, by Ethel Snowden, namely: that woman's invasion of the gainful occupations appears to be found unwomanly in proportion to the importance of the position to which she aspires.

It is the married woman in business or in professional work, as it is in industry, who suffers most from the surviving prejudices concerning her sex. When there are economies to be effected through the discharge of workers, the idea that the married woman is normally a dependent comes immediately to the fore, and she is the first employee to be discharged. For example, *Equal Rights* of 8 August, 1925, noted in an editorial that the city of St. Louis had begun a campaign for economy by discharging twelve married women; that there was a movement on in Germany to reduce governmental expenses by a wholesale discharge of women employees; and that, according to rumour, Mr. Coolidge's campaign of economy was being made to bear most heavily on married women. The comment of *Equal Rights* on the action of the city of St. Louis is worth quoting:

St. Louis employed twenty-seven married women. It investigated the economic condition of all these, retained nine, discharged twelve, and was, at last report, still considering the case of the other six. St. Louis did not investigate the economic condition of the men employees, to see whether or not these might continue to live if they were discharged. St. Louis did not try to find out whether or not these men had fathers, brothers, mothers, or wives who might support them while they were looking for other jobs. St. Louis assumed that men have a right to economic independence and the increased happiness and opportunity that it brings. St. Louis assumed that women have no such right.

In other words, St. Louis assumed, as the German and American Governments apparently assume, and as most private employers assume, that women are employed on sufferance; especially married women. Of course it should be remembered that the position of the married woman in this respect is only worse than that of single women, and that the position of women is only worse than that of men; for, as I have already remarked, under a monopolistic economic system the opportunity to earn a living by one's labour comes to be regarded as a privilege instead of a natural right. Women are simply held to be less entitled to this privilege than men.

That marriage should so often assume the nature of a disability for the woman who either wishes or is obliged to earn, whereas it often operates in favour of the male worker, may be attributed to the traditional assumption that married women are dependent on, and subject to, their husbands. I remarked in the preceding chapter that the married woman who wishes to engage in business finds herself, in many communities, hampered by legal disabilities arising from her marital status, whereas her husband is under no corresponding disabilities. Her position as an industrial and salaried worker is rendered insecure if not by law, at least by the same psychology that keeps legal disabilities in force. This psychology may be defined as the expectation that a woman when she marries shall surrender a much greater degree of personal freedom than the man she marries. The man who does not object to his wife's having a career is considered generous and long-suffering. His insistence on her abandoning it and contenting herself with looking out for his domestic comfort is thought to be quite natural.[1] On the other hand, the woman

[1] There are, of course, exceptions to this rule; as when a woman has, before her marriage, already made a great reputation. In such a case the husband would be thought selfish who demanded the sacrifice of her career. But the husband who demands the sacrifice of a potential career is generally thought to be well within his rights.

who interferes in any way with a husband's career is regarded as an extremely selfish person; while any sacrifice of herself and her ambitions to her husband and his, is thought of merely as a matter of wifely duty. How often does one hear that such and such a woman has given up her position because "her husband didn't want her to work." There is, too, a very general assumption that every married woman has children and should stay at home and take care of them. Now, perhaps every married woman should have children; perhaps in a future state of society men and women will marry only when they wish to bring up a family. But at present it is not so; therefore at present the assumption that a married woman should stay at home and take care of her children leaves out of account the fact that a large and increasing number of married women are childless. It may be contended that these women should stay at home and take care of their husbands; but even if we assume that the unremitting personal attention of his wife is essential to the comfort and happiness of a married man, there would still remain the question of his title to this attention at the cost of her own interests.

We are dealing here with an attitude which, gen-

Economic Position of Women

eral though it be, has been outmoded by the conditions of modern life. The sexual division of interests and labour which has been insisted upon so long among European peoples does not very well fit in with the organization of industrial and social life in the twentieth century. Our social ideology, like our political ideology, is of the eighteenth century; and its especial effectiveness at present is by way of obscuring our vision of the changed world that has emerged from the great economic revolution of the last century. A division of interests and labour which was convenient if not just under the conditions of economic and social life which preceded the industrial revolution, is neither convenient nor just under the conditions which prevail today. The care of young children and the management of a household may result in an unequal division of labour in families where the husband's inability to provide for the needs of his family forces the wife to assume the burdens of a breadwinner. When one reads through the literature on the question of hours of labour for women in industry, one is struck by the persistent stressing of the married woman's double burden of breadwinning and housekeeping. These women, it seems, must not only earn money to contribute to their families' support, but they must, before setting out for work and after returning from it, prepare the family meals, get the children ready for school or the day-nursery, take them there and call for them, wash, sew, and perform a hundred other household tasks. This double burden is often made an argument for establishing shorter hours of work for women in industry, but never for expecting the husband to share the wife's traditional burden as she has been forced to share his. I have no doubt that innumerable husbands are doing this; but there is no expectation put upon them to do it, and those who do not are in no wise thought to shirk their duty to their families, as their wives would be thought to do if they neglected to perform the labour of the household.

Quite analogous to this attitude of the advocates of special legislation for working women is that of the people who concern themselves with the so-called problem of the educated woman, which is supposed to be that of reconciling domesticity with intellectual pursuits. A timely illustration of this attitude is the establishment by Smith College of an institute for the "co-ordination of women's interests." The purpose of this institute, in the words of President Neilson, is "to find a solution of the problem which confronts almost every educated woman today—how to reconcile a normal life of marriage and motherhood with a life of intellectual activity, professional or otherwise." Here again is the tacit assumption that marriage is the special concern of woman, and one whose claims must take precedence over her other interests, whatever they may be; that marriage and motherhood constitute her normal life, and her other interests something extra-normal which must somehow be made to fit in if possible. I have heard of no institute intended to find a way to reconcile the normal life of marriage and fatherhood with a life of intellectual activity, professional or otherwise; although when one considers how many educated men of today are obliged to compromise with their consciences in order to secure themselves in positions which will enable them to provide for their families, one is persuaded that some such institute might be at least equally appropriate and equally helpful with that which Smith College has established.

Let us forget for a moment the sophisticated traditional attitude toward this question of marriage and parenthood, and go back, as it were, to the beginning—to a fact recognized in the animal world and not entirely overlooked by primitive man, namely: that every offspring has two parents who are equally responsible for its care and protection. In the animal kingdom one finds a widely varied division of the labour connected with the care of the young. For example, the male of certain species is found to perform functions which our own usage has led us to regard as maternal. Among the viviparous animals the heavier share of responsibility rests with the female during the gestation, birth and extreme youth of the offspring; and among primitive human beings the actual physical dependence of the offspring on the mother is likely to be prolonged over a period of several years. It was, perhaps, this necessity of a close physical association between mother and child that led to a sexual division of labour under which the mother undertook the physical care of children while the father undertook the task of providing food. It must be remarked, however, that this division of labour by no means excludes productive labour on the part of the woman. Among most tribes she augments the food-supply through agriculture, grubbing, or sometimes through

Economic Position of Women 197

fishing or hunting; and there are tribes, notably in Africa, where she is the sole provider for the family. The Vaertings have remarked that the drudgery connected with the care of children is invariably imposed by the dominant upon the subject sex; a view which is in perfect consonance with what we know of the general human willingness to transfer to other shoulders the burden of uninteresting though necessary labour. Since women have most often been subject, they have most often been forced to undertake this drudgery, either in lieu of or in addition to the labour of providing food and shelter for their families.

This is to say that their subject position has added considerably to what newspaper editors and other commentators are fond of calling the burden of Eve. Since woman is the childbearing sex, it has seemed natural to a great many peoples to increase the disadvantage at which her share in reproduction naturally places her, by making her confinement at home permanent instead of occasional, and by permitting her few, if any, interests save those connected with reproduction; in short, by prolonging and enhancing her subjection to the demands of the race. This is why the term married woman is still taken to imply the term housekeeper; an implication which, as the *Freeman* remarked editorially some years ago, modern civilization must renounce "if it wants such of its women as are editors and bank-presidents to be mothers as well."

Civilization shortens the period of the child's physical dependence on the mother by shortening the period of lactation. On the other hand, it increases fecundity to such an extent that where religious superstition or ignorance prevents the use of contraceptives, the burden of childbearing is greatly increased. This result of civilization is not, however, commonly found among the educated classes; and even among those classes where children are most numerous, I have already shown that women are not restrained by motherhood from engaging in gainful occupations outside the home. On the contrary, the number of their offspring is more often their chief incentive to this course. Among well-to-do families, prepared foods and wet-nursing have for a long time been rather generally employed to relieve mothers even of the responsibility of lactation, while the custom of assigning the physical care of children to hired substitutes has reduced their actual work to that of bringing the child into the world. That this mode of caring for children is approved by all classes is evident from their readiness to adopt it when fortune favours them with an opportunity. It is occasionally inveighed against by moralists, but on the whole it is coveted and approved, especially while women devote to frivolous pursuits the leisure that it leaves them. When a woman adopts this mode in order to reconcile motherhood with a serious interest outside the home, it is a different matter, and lays her open to the charge of neglecting her family, though in fact she may spend no more hours away from home than the woman who gives her morning to shopping and her afternoon to playing bridge. Why this should be the case I am at a loss to know, unless it be that a serious interest outside the home appears to smack too much of an assertion of her right to live her life for her own sake rather than for the sake of the race or that of her husband—a self-assertion not readily to be accepted without such reservations as find expression in institutes designed to "co-ordinate women's interests."

It appears, then, that the care of the young is the concern of both sexes, and is so recognized in the animal world and among human beings; and that among the latter such differences in usage as exist touching this matter are differences in the apportioning of the burden. Even in our own day, when there is observable a tendency to forget that the child has more than one parent—that parent being the mother—the father's claim to his children is still recognized in law, often to the prejudice of the mother's; and so, likewise, is his obligation to provide for them. Indeed, the child may be said to be regarded as exclusively the mother's only while it is young; for it is a general custom among us to speak of Mrs. So-and-So's baby, but of Mr. So-and-So's son or daughter. Let us, then, recognize the claim and interest of both parents. Let us also remember that the economic organization has so extensively altered that the traditional division of labour—this division is always profoundly affected by consideration of the young—has been outmoded as far as thousands of families are concerned. Let us also assume that woman has established her right to be considered as a human being rather than a function or a chattel. Then it must seem reasonable to assume that the co-ordination of interests to be brought about concerns both sexes equally; that the problem to be confronted is that of reconciling

Economic Position of Women 201

a normal life of marriage and parenthood not only with the freest possible development of intellectual interest but with the utmost devotion to any chosen profession.

I can not pretend to foretell how this problem will be settled; for its solution will depend upon the general solution of the labour-problem. It may be that the necessary collectivism of modern industry will result in a collectivist system of caring for children. Such a system would by no means be an innovation; it would simply constitute an extension and adaptation of means which already exist—of nurseries for very small children and schools for older ones. Whatever its demerits might be, such a system would certainly represent an enormous economy of effort. The average home is adapted less to the needs of children than to those of adults; hence a mother of young children must spend a great deal of her time in preventing her young charges from injuring themselves with dangerous household implements, from falling downstairs or off of furniture too high for them, and from touching objects which would not be safe in their hands. In a properly equipped nursery, on the other hand, the furniture and all the objects are adapted to the size and intelligence of the children. Children have the advantage of numerous playmates; and one person can supervise the play of a dozen of them with less fatigue than the mother of one is likely to feel at the end of a day in the average home.

The Russians have already taken some steps in this direction by establishing both nurseries and schools in connexion with certain factories. From what I can gather of their policy, it would seem that they regard the care and education of children as being very much the concern of the whole community. They look upon childbearing as a service to the community, but they do not appear to take the view that women should be required to perform this service at the expense of their independence, for they have instituted a system of subsidies for pregnant and nursing working mothers, with rest-periods before and after confinement, and a subsidy during confinement amounting to the daily subsidy multiplied by fifteen.[1]

I have already indicated in the preceding chapter

[1] From the Laws and Decrees of the Soviet Government on medical questions, sanitation, etc., published in Moscow, 1922.

what it seems to me would be the course of a free people in this matter of reconciling the care of children with the greatest possible freedom for both parents. It seems hardly necessary to call attention to the obvious fact that the question is simply that of placing the care of the young in the hands of those who are interested in it and fitted for it, instead of forcing it willy-nilly upon either sex through a traditional expectation and a traditional division of labour. In a free society, those parents who wished to pursue careers incompatible with the actual care of young children would avail themselves of the services of substitutes, as the well-to-do classes do at present; and they might do so with even greater confidence because, as I have remarked, those engaged in caring for and teaching the young would do so as a matter of interest primarily and only secondarily as a means of livelihood. There is another important consideration to be taken into account, and that is, that in a free society the problem of reconciling the occupations of the parents with their personal supervision of their children would be much easier to solve; for their hours of labour would be greatly decreased. It is only where production must support an enormous amount of idleness and waste that it is necessary to overwork producers.

It is possible, of course, that the institution of economic freedom might check the present tendency of women to engage in gainful occupations outside the home. It most certainly would if the vast increase of opportunity which it offered were reserved exclusively for men; but to bring about this result it would be necessary for traditional anti-feminist prejudices to survive much more strongly than they do today. The position of women has too radically changed to admit of their exclusion from direct participation in the benefits of economic freedom; therefore if they resigned the increased economic opportunities that it offered them, and withdrew to the sphere of domesticity, they would do so as a matter of choice. Why should we not expect them to choose the exclusive domesticity which might be rendered possible through the increased earning power of men? They probably would, where it suited their taste to do so; but one of the most powerful incentives to do so would no longer exist, namely: the desire for economic security. Women, to be sure, are not exempt from the characteristic willingness of humankind to live by the exertions of others; but I would remark that there is this difference between the person who does this indirectly, through legalized privilege, and the person who depends directly on the bounty of another: that the former is independent and the latter is dependent. Women are not strangers to the human desire for freedom; and when the fear of want is allayed they are quite likely to prefer an easy and secure self-support to the alternative of economic dependence. Moreover, economic freedom would set domesticity in competition with the interests of women rather than their needs; for it would set all people free to engage in occupations that interested them, whereas at present the vast majority do whatever offers them a living. Under these circumstances it might reasonably be expected that the number of women who would continue in business and in industrial and professional pursuits, even after marriage and the birth of children, would greatly increase.

Indeed, if we postulate an economic system under which every human being would be free to choose his occupation in accordance with his interests, I see no more reason to suppose that women would invariably choose domesticity than to suppose that all men would choose blacksmithing. Under such a régime I doubt that even the power of the expected which affects them so strongly at present, would long continue in an effectiveness which it has already begun to lose. Women, I think, might be expected to choose their occupations with the same freedom as men, and to look for no serious interruption from marriage and the birth of children. There are a good many women at present who very ably reconcile motherhood with a chosen career. I think we might expect to find more of them rather than fewer, in a free society. One thing is certain, and it is the important thing: they would be free to choose. If it be woman's nature, as some people still believe, to wish to live at second hand, then in a free society they will freely make that choice, and no one can complain of it—unless it be the men on whom they elect to depend. However, to assume from past experience that they do want to live at second hand is to assume that all the social and legal injustices which have been employed to force them to do so, were unnecessary; and when have Governments and communities wasted their power in exercising compulsion where no compulsion was needed?

CHAPTER VI

WHAT IS TO BE DONE

I

IN the foregoing chapters I have intimated that every phase of the question of freedom for women is bound up with the larger question of human freedom. If it is freedom that women want, they can not be content to be legally equal with men; but having gained this equality they must carry on their struggle against the oppressions which privilege exercises upon humanity at large by virtue of an usurped economic power. All human beings, presumably, would gain by freedom; but women particularly stand to gain by it, for as I have shown, they are victims of special prepossessions which mere legal equality with men may hardly be expected to affect.

If, on the other hand, it is dominance that they desire, they might, indeed, conceivably attain this without freedom; but one can not see much encouragement for that wish in the present trend of affairs. Before women could dominate, they would not only have to overcome the prejudices, superstitions, and legal disabilities which have contributed to their subjection; but they would also have to get the upper hand of men economically. They would have to manœuvre themselves into that advantage in opportunity which men at present enjoy. One can hardly see how this could be brought about except by some kind of *coup d'état,* for the tendency of modern legislation, as I have shown, far from being calculated to enlarge the scope of women's economic activity, is likely rather to narrow it; nor is it entirely probable that the establishment of mere legal equality would count for much in the premises, for the courts may always decide that any legislation designed for the Larger Good is valid even though it may clash with the principle of equal rights.[1] Suppose, however, that the momentum gathered by the woman's movement should carry society through a period of sex-equality and bring it out on the other side—the side of female domina-

---

[1] Still, putting the shoe on the other foot, there is no denying that discriminative legislation based on the Larger Good might as well serve to secure to women privileges which would lead toward female domination, as to create disabilities which would keep them at a disadvantage compared with men. Even the United States Supreme Court has been known to reverse itself.

tion—then men and women would simply have exchanged places, and the social evils which now afflict mankind would remain, *mutatis mutandis*. Women would be more nearly free than men, as men are now more nearly free than women; but no one would be really free, because real freedom is not a matter of the shifting of advantage from one sex to the other or from one class to another. Real freedom means the disappearance of advantage, and primarily of economic advantage. It can not be too often repeated that political and social freedom are unattainable unless and until economic freedom has been attained—but this is not a concern of either sex or class. In order to live, women, like men, must eat; to eat, they, like men, must labour; to labour, they, like men, must have opportunity. Control of men's and women's economic opportunity, therefore, means control of their livelihood, and control of men's and women's livelihood means control of men and women. Real freedom, therefore, does not come in sight of either men or women until this control is abated; that is to say, until (speaking in technical terms) the two active factors in production, capital and labour, which are *pro tanto* sexless, have free access to the passive factor, natural resources—in other words, until the private monopoly of natural resources is dissolved.

If the struggle of women to rid themselves of their peculiar disabilities were to turn out into an attempt to dominate men as men have for so long dominated women, one could perfectly understand the psychology behind such an attempt. With the exception of a few individuals, humankind has thus far achieved no very high idea of freedom. The ambition of subject classes has never gone much beyond the desire to enjoy the privileges usurped by their masters. They have resented being dominated, but not domination; they have had no repugnance to the thought of dominating others. Their psychology was very well summed up by *Punch*, in the remark of one old market-woman to another (I quote from memory): "You see, Mrs. ——, when we have a Labour Government we'll all be equal, and then I shall have a servant to do my work for me." It is because of this myopic view of the nature of freedom that all revolutions have been mere scrambles for advantage, and have accomplished nothing more than a shifting of power from one class to another, or as John Adams said,

What Is To Be Done

"a mere change of impostors." If the woman's movement should resolve itself into a similar scramble, it would be unfortunate but not surprising, for women may hardly be expected to rise at once above the retaliatory spirit which is one of the common curses of humanity.

They would have good *ex parte* arguments ready to their tongue; many an argument, indeed, which has been advanced to defend their subjection might be effectively turned around. Their part in parenthood for example, has long been held to justify their subjection under the guise of protection in this function. It would be equally logical to argue that women, as mothers of the race, should dominate the family because, as givers of life, they have a deeper personal interest and a greater natural right in their children than men have. It might be argued that they should control all public affairs because of the greater understanding of the value of human life and deeper interest in the welfare of humanity that motherhood brings. One often hears the argument —which no amount of female bloodthirst in time of war ever seems to make effectively ridiculous— that if women were in power there would be no wars, because they, knowing the cost of giving life, would not consent to its wilful wholesale destruction. The doctrine that women are closer to the race than men is really dangerous to those who now preach it; for it affords the best kind of basis for the contention that women should dominate in all matters concerning the race—and all human affairs may be held to concern the race in one way or another.

Perhaps the best argument for the domination of women is that if society, like parliamentary government, must for ever contemplate a mere sterile succession of outs and ins, it is time that women had their innings. But the analogy with the parliamentary system goes further. Public faith in the parliamentary principle has waned almost to the disappearing-point, and the system has suffered wholesale discredit, because it became slowly but surely evident that what actually kept them up was "the cohesive power of public plunder." If women took what might be called by analogy the political view of their right to their innings, and let it animate them in a scuffle for predominance, the general reaction would be similar. In a matter of this kind, great numbers of people would be found objective enough to glance at such an effort and pass it by in disapproval of the waste of energy involved in bringing about a readjustment that promised nothing better than a shifting of the incidence of injustice. Women would thus forfeit a great deal of sympathy, and at the same time probably create even more antagonism than they have thus far had to face. They would place themselves in a position similar to that of organized labour, which is so intent on contending for what it conceives to be its own interest—a position of advantage in bargaining on wages and conditions of labour—that by the narrowness of its policy it antagonizes a great deal of public sentiment which must inevitably be enlisted on its behalf if it undertook to contend for the general interest, in which its own is included, and in the service of which its own is bound, in the long run, to be best served.

What the nature of this general interest is, I have already intimated. It is economic, and it can be advanced only through the establishment of an order of society in which every human being shall enjoy the natural right to labour and to enjoy all that his labour produces. It is upon mankind's security in this right that human freedom, in whatever mode or aspect—social, philosophical, political, religious—primarily depends.

The right to labour and to enjoy the fruits of one's labour means only the right of free access to the source of subsistence, which is land.[1] If access to that source may be arbitrarily denied, the right to labour is denied, and the opportunity to get one's living becomes a privilege which may be withheld or granted as suits the need or convenience of the person who bestows it, and wholly on his own terms. If access may be had only on the payment of tribute, the condition abrogates the right to enjoy the fruit of one's labour, for the tribute consumes a share of it.

While access to land is free, no one need know want; for he may always get his living by applying his labour to natural resources "on his own." He may always, that is, work for himself instead of depending for his living on the chance to work for an employer. Under such conditions, moreover, no one need content himself, as the labourer is forced to content himself at present, with a small

---

[1] Land, that is, in the technical economic sense. It does not mean the solid part of the earth's surface—earth as distinguished from water. It means the sum-total of natural resources.

share of what his labour produces, for as Turgot pointed out a century and a half ago, he can always demand of an employer the full equivalent of what he could earn by working for himself. It is clear that under such an economic system, the share of the capitalist in any product would amount only to a fair competitive return on his actual investment. Under the present system the capitalist often enjoys both directly and indirectly the advantage of monopoly, which enables him to appropriate an unfair proportion of his workers' labour-product. He is a direct beneficiary of monopoly when he holds legal title to the source of his product—cultivable land, mines, forests, water-power—or where he holds franchises or profits by protective tariffs or embargoes. He is an indirect beneficiary when he profits by the competition for work among workers whom monopoly has deprived of free access to land. The steel-trust, as I have remarked, is a striking example of a capitalist organization which benefits both directly and indirectly by monopoly. On the one hand, it monopolizes and holds out of access vast mining-properties, and monopolizes the home market through a protective tariff. On the other, it levies tribute on labour by virtue of the scarcity of opportunity created by monopoly in general.

Another excellent instance of this dual advantage is furnished by the railways of this country. Not only have they received governmental land-grants worth enough to cover their construction-costs many times over, but they hold a valuable franchise-monopoly in the exclusive right to do business over a long continuous strip of land called their "right of way"; by means of which monopoly they drain the commerce of a vast area as a river drains its waters. Through the enormous wealth which these monopolies have enabled them to accumulate, they have been able to influence governmental policy in ways designed to enhance their privileges; for example, they have been able to curtail water-transportation and thus reduce competition. They have profited by tariffs, as through the emergency-law some years ago, which raised the tariff on wheat just enough to cover the difference between the cost of landing a bushel of wheat from the Argentine at one of our Eastern ports, and the rate for transporting it by railway from our Western wheat-fields. Through the Interstate Commerce Commission, of which they cap-

What Is To Be Done

tured control almost as soon as it was formed, they are allowed to levy rates which represent not the cost of transportation but the amount which can be exacted for it. So much for their direct benefit from monopoly. Indirectly they benefit in the same way as any other capitalist, through the opportunity to exploit a labour-surplus created and maintained by monopoly; and while they are somewhat hindered in making the most of this opportunity by the effectiveness of defensive organization among their skilled employees, they have a pretty free hand with their thousands of unskilled workers, and manage on the whole to do very well out of them.

Even where the capitalist is not himself to any significant extent a monopolist, he derives great benefit from monopoly, for it is thanks to the monopolist of natural resources that he is able to keep labourers at, or very near, the margin of subsistence. He is not always, however, undisturbed in the enjoyment of his advantage; for he may be himself quite as much at the mercy of monopoly as the workers he exploits. The tenant-farmer affords an excellent example of this. He is the capitalist in the farming-industry, who pays to the land-monopolist tribute in the form of rent, to the railways tribute in exorbitant freight-rates on his implements and products, to the manufacturers of his implements tribute in the form of tariffs. He furnishes the capital necessary for operating the farm, pays the wages of such labour as he may require, and takes for himself what is left after all these charges have been met, which in this country is so little that it does not suffice to pay him both interest on his capital and wages for his own labour—a condition which explains the steady drift of our population from the farms to the cities, and which also accounts for the extraordinary fact that agriculture, which is in volume our greatest industry is, *qua* industry, bankrupt. All the money in farming is now, and for some time has been, in the rise of landvalues. It is evident, then, that save where capital and monopoly are united, capital as well as labour is victimized by monopoly. This is one of the most important facts of our system, and almost everyone overlooks it. The whole producing organization is levied upon by a power which itself performs no service whatever in return for the wealth that it appropriates; which is, on the contrary, an incubus on the producing organization. To put this

What Is To Be Done 219

statement more clearly, the monopolist, whose control of the sources of production makes his exactions inescapable, is limited in those exactions only by the amount that the traffic will bear. If a condition arises which makes a certain kind of production especially desirable, there will naturally be a pressure of people desiring to undertake that kind of production, and the monopolist who controls its source will exact in payment for access to that source an amount fixed by the number of competitors seeking access. He is thus able to absorb all the returns of the industry which depends on his monopoly, except just so much as is necessary to encourage people to keep on with it. For example, during the war the owners of our Western wheat-lands, who had been demanding one-third of the crop in rent, raised the amount to two-fifths, because at the price fixed by the Government wheat-growing was profitable and there were many would-be producers seeking access to wheat-lands. The same condition was reflected in the selling price of land. Farms were sold and resold at advancing prices until land that had sold before the war for sixty-five dollars an acre was bringing two hundred. During the period of deflation thousands of acres bought on mortgages reverted from one buyer to another until the original owner had back his land plus whatever profit he had had from its sale. All this raising of rents and this buying and selling at inflated prices, did nothing for production, obviously, except to drain off the lion's share of its proceeds into the pocket of the monopolist; for all speculative values must necessarily be paid finally out of production, since there is no other source for them to come from. The producing organization thus carries an enormous load of people who draw their living from it and give neither goods nor services in return; who live, that is to say, by appropriating the labour-products of others without compensation—in other words, by legalized theft.

As monopoly extends and tightens its grip on the sources of production, it is enabled to exact an increasing share of the proceeds, until the point is reached where industry can no longer meet its demands and continue to pay interest and wages. For example, so long as this country had a frontier, the monopolist was in no position to exact a very great share of production, for the producer had the alternative of pushing on to the margin of cultivation where there were as yet no landlords to support.

The monopolist, therefore, could exact no more than the difference between what a man might earn in a sparsely settled country, remote from markets, and what he could earn by carrying on production in a more thickly settled and more nearly monopolized region. So long as this condition endured, production in this country was able to pay tribute to monopoly and still pay the capitalist a fairly good rate of interest and the labourer a fairly good wage. But since the late nineteenth century, when the frontier was closed, all the best of the country's land and natural resources being legally occupied, monopoly has been able to exact an ever greater share of production; for while monopoly progresses, the population grows, and competitive demand for access to the source of production increases; and these two causes combine to cut down free economic opportunity to the disappearing point. Thus it seems only a matter of time until production will break down under the exactions of monopoly and revolution and readjustment will follow. The breakdown has already begun in the basic industry, agriculture, for, as I have stated above, the tenant farmer is no longer able to meet the charges of monopoly and still earn interest and wages. Therefore our agrarian population, literally starved off the land, is steadily drifting to the cities, to swell the numbers of workers who crowd the industrial labour-market. This is to say that our civilization is dying at the root; and this having presently grown too rotten to nourish it or support it, a little wind of revolution or foreign invasion will one day overturn it, as all civilizations which have hitherto existed have been overturned by the same cause. "*Latifundia,*" said Pliny, "*perdiderunt Romam.*"

This same economic system exists in all the great countries of the world save Russia, where it broke down under the Czarist régime and has not been re-established. It is farther advanced in the countries of the old world than it is here, because this country is more recently settled. This fact constitutes the only difference between the economic order in the old world and that in the new—a difference in the degree that exploitation has reached.

Wherever exploitation exists, whether in the new world or the old, it exists by means of a governmental organization which its beneficiaries control and use to protect their privileges against the expropriated and exploited masses. There is general agreement among scholars that in government, exploitation came first, and what we know as law and order are its incidental by-products; and that however far the development of these by-products may go, they are never allowed to interfere with exploitation. "The State," says Oppenheimer, "grew from the subjugation of one group of men by another. Its basic justification, its *raison d'être*, was and is the economic exploitation of those subjugated." Both the origin and the essential nature of the State remain perfectly clear so long as the conquering class remains distinct from the subject classes and keeps these in a state of vassalage, without freedom of movement, and subject to transfer from one owner to another along with the land on which they dwell. In our own age, they are quite evident in the dealings of the Western powers with weak peoples, as in India or the Philippine Islands, or the mandated territories under the League of Nations, where foreign Governments, through their military organizations, protect their nationals in an economic exploitation of the native population, and themselves levy taxes upon the natives to pay the costs of the process. The nature and purpose of the State are clear, indeed, in any community where the owning and exploiting class exercises direct control over the propertyless dependent classes as more or less chattels. The landed aristocracy of Europe formerly exercised this direct control, as their titles, now grown meaningless, indicate.

But where the form of the State has undergone a change which precludes this direct control by the owning class, the nature of the State, and its essential function, are obscured. Under the republicanism which succeeded the American and French revolutions, the expropriated classes have gained freedom of movement, a limited freedom of opinion, and a nominal share in the exercise of government. The peasant is no longer bound to the soil he tills; he may leave it at will to seek his fortune elsewhere —on the terms of another landlord. The owning classes no longer directly exercise government or directly enjoy honours and titles by virtue of ownership. The peoples of the Western world, at least where parliamentarism has not broken down, have a nominal freedom with little of the reality. Nominal freedom of movement is worth little to the man who faces the alternative of being exploited where he is, or being exploited elsewhere. Nominal freedom of opinion is not extremely valuable when expression of opinion may cost one the opportunity to earn one's living; and the right to vote offers little satisfaction when it means merely a right of choice between rival parties and candidates representing exactly the same system of economic exploitation.

The political revolution which followed the breakdown of feudalism did the world its greatest service in launching the *idea* of freedom; it did nothing—or relatively very little—for its substance. Through its agency the equal right of all human beings to "life, liberty, and the pursuit of happiness" has come to be granted in theory though not in fact; it remained for the Russian Revolution to proclaim the further idea that the basis of this right is not political but economic. The political revolution did more; by establishing political democracy, it put into the hands of the people the power to achieve economic democracy by peaceful means. But by that very act it obscured the essential function of the State and the source of its power, which remained clear as long as those who owned ruled directly by virtue of ownership; and thus it hindered a clear perception of the causal relation between privilege and slavery. By abolishing hereditary power, it effected a redistribution of privilege, and at the same time forced privilege to exercise its control of government by indirect means. Privilege was no longer seated on the throne, but it remained, through its control of economic opportunity, the power behind the throne;[1] a power all the more difficult to dislodge now that it exercised control without assuming responsibility. Republicanism has proved the futility of dislodging a privileged class without abolishing privilege; for this simply prepares the way for the rise of a new privileged class which will use government to enforce its exploitation of the propertyless class, in a different way, perhaps, but quite as effectively as its predecessors.

The psychological effect of the political equality established under republicanism is extremely demoralizing. As I have remarked, the subject classes have never desired freedom so much as a chance at the privileges that they see other people enjoy. Political equality, with its breaking-down of class distinctions, creates an impression of equality of opportunity—and indeed to the extent that government maintains no disabling legal discriminations

---

[1] It is hardly necessary to go into the methods by which this control is exercised. In a country where government is elected, as in this, privilege controls through its contribution to party-funds, through bribery, through economic pressure, and all the other means which its control of economic opportunity puts at its disposal.

What Is To Be Done 227

among members of the enfranchised class,[1] it actually establishes equality. No member of that class is excluded from the benefits of privilege by anything save his inability to get possession of it; and this fact, especially in a country where opportunity is comparatively plentiful, is more likely to confirm people in their loyalty to a system under which they stand even a dog's chance to become beneficiaries of privilege, than it is to stimulate an endeavour to abolish privilege altogether. In this country the incalculable richness of natural resources and the enormous wealth to be gained by speculative enterprise under a government which gives full rein to monopoly, contributed immensely to the corruption of the citizenry. Speculation became the normal course of enterprise, the most approved method of money-getting; and the more ruinously did the monopolist exploit the country's resources, as Mr. Veblen has pointed out, the greater the regard in which he was held by his fellow citizens. Never before in the world's history had so many people a chance at the enjoyment of privilege as in the pioneer

---

[1] Women and slaves were discriminated against in this country; and in the State of California today, no person incapable of citizenship may hold land—a provision which excludes Japanese and Chinese.

period of American development. The country's resources were gutted for profit, not developed for use. The use-value of land was incidental to its value as real estate. Every farmer became a speculator, and consequently the margin of cultivation, instead of being pushed out gradually in response to the natural increase in the country's needs, was extended artificially and with extreme rapidity, with the result that farms were miles apart and unnecessary difficulties in marketing, and in the maintenance of education and social life, were created. The country resembled the modern city-addition of the real-estater, with all the framework of settlement, waiting for the pressure of population to enhance the selling-price of land. Not only was the public mind corrupted by the apparently limitless opportunity to enjoy privilege—not only was speculation confused with production—but all this opportunity was blindly attributed to the blessings of republicanism. "The greatest government on earth" came to be regarded as the guardian of free opportunity for all citizens, in spite of the very evident fact that no government which protects land-monopoly can possibly maintain freedom of opportunity, for in the course of monopoly all available natural resources are

What Is To Be Done 229

shortly pre-empted, and those people who are born after occupation is complete will find nothing left to pre-empt. Thus American patriotism took on a religious fervour, and the corruption of the populace was complete.

The rise of industrialism has done as much as anything else to engender misapprehension of the State's essential nature, its chief function, and the source of its power. It is significant that the Physiocrats lived and observed the workings of the State before the industrial era, in an agricultural country, where the relation between land-monopoly and government was direct and inescapable; and that Karl Marx lived and wrote after the rise of the factory-system, in a highly industrialized country. The Physiocrats, for whom the basic economic problem was unobscured, therefore attributed involuntary poverty to its actual cause; while Marx, confusing capital's fortuitous advantage from monopoly with monopoly itself, laid the responsibility at the door of capitalism. To be sure, Marx recognized and stated the fact that expropriation must precede exploitation; but he did not draw the obvious conclusion that the way to break capital's power to exploit the worker is by simple reimpropriation. At present there is a general impression that the factory-system lured the population into the cities, and thus caused the overcrowding that results in scarcity of jobs and inadequacy of wage. As a matter of fact, the factory-system found the cities already overcrowded with exploitable labour. In England, for example, the Enclosures Acts had deprived the people of what common land remained to them, and had driven them into the cities where they lived in inconceivable filth and squalor, eking out a miserable existence under the old family-system of industry. The machine-system found all this expropriated and exploitable human material ready to serve its ends —far more, indeed, than it needed, as the riots among the workers deprived of their livelihood by its labour-saving tools, plainly indicated. The industrial revolution, then, did not produce the overcrowding of the labour-market; but the capitalist of the revolution profited by an overcrowding that already existed. He reaped indirectly the fruits of monopoly. He profited likewise, and profits still, by every labour-saving device, for it enabled him at once to dispense with some labourers and, because of the increase of unemployment thus caused, to pay his remaining workers less. Capital was thus enabled to appropriate much more than its rightful share of production, and hence to amass enormous wealth, by means of which it influenced government on behalf of its own further enrichment. In this country, it has secured a system of protective tariffs which amount to a governmental delegation of taxing-power to the protected industries; it gives them a monopoly of the home-market and enables them to add to the price of their product the amount of the tariff which has been set against the competing foreign article. Capital has found other ways of creating monopolies, such as the combinations in restraint of trade at which the ineffectual Sherman law was levelled. As the exactions of monopoly increase, and the exploitation of labour nears the point of diminishing return, the capitalist-monopolist embarks, with the protection of government, on a policy of economic imperialism. He monopolizes the markets of weak nations at the point of his Government's bayonets. He invests in foreign enterprises which offer high returns for himself and risk of war for the Government which backs him—that is to say, for the exploited masses at home who must support the Government and furnish its soldiers. In short, he constitutes himself a menace to peace and prosperity both at home and abroad; so that it is not to be wondered at if people observing his sinister activities, take capital to be the cause of the economic injustice from which it derives its power. Yet, if natural resources were put freely in competition with industry for the employment of labour, the inflamed fortunes of the capitalist class would disappear. Monoply having been abolished,[1] the capitalist-monopolist would no longer exist, and the capitalist would no longer be in a position to exact from production anything more than his rightful interest—that is, as I have said, the amount fixed by free competitive demand for the use of his capital.

There is yet another cause of confusion in the long-established custom of regarding land as private property, whereas it is not, rightly speaking, private property at all, but the source from which property

[1] A great deal is said about credit-monopoly, as if it were something requiring a new and special kind of instrument to break up. But what is credit? Merely a device for facilitating the exchange of wealth, and all wealth is produced from land. The break-up of land-monopoly would therefore at once break up credit-monopoly. Or, putting it in another way, the one and only imperishable security is land—all other forms of security finally run back to it. The break-up of land-monopoly would therefore break up the monopoly of all the secondary and derived forms of security upon which credit could be based.

is produced by the combined efforts of labour and capital. The right to property in wealth which has been produced, as, for instance, the coat on one's back, may be defended on the ground that it is the product of one's own labour, or has been acquired through exchange of an equivalent amount of one's own product; but the right to property in land can not be defended on the same ground, because land is not a labour-product. The distinction is simply between labour-made property and law-made property. Under our present system of tenure, to be sure, the purchase price of land—that is, the investment of capital that the owner has made in order to get title—may represent human labour—but this is merely to say that the owner has invested his capital in privilege, or law-made property; that he has purchased, under governmental guarantee, a certain delegation of taxing-power, precisely as the investor in governmental securities purchases a governmental guarantee that a certain share of future labour-products will be taken from the producers and turned over to him. The fact that, under political government, capital may be invested in privilege in no wise alters the iniquitous nature of privilege, and a sound public policy would disallow an investor's plea of good faith *ex post facto*.[1] Under a system which did not permit such investments, those people who wished to put their capital to gainful use would invest it in the only legitimate way, which is in productive enterprise.

It is, perhaps, partly because of the confusion of thought produced by all these causes, that no revolution has ever abolished the exploiting State and the privileges that it exists to secure. But it must also be remembered that all revolutions have risen out of factional disputes or class-wars, and that in the latter case, the chief interest of the revolting class has been not to abolish privilege but to redistribute it. The French Revolution, for instance, expropriated the land-owning nobility, but its politicians dared not abolish private land-monopoly, for the bourgeoisie which supported the revolution would not have tolerated such an interference with their own enjoyment of privilege. In one important respect the Russian Revolution is an exception to this rule. It is a class-revolution, but its avowed ultimate purpose

---

[1] There is recent precedent for this in American law. Under the XVIII Amendment and the Volstead Act, the Federal Government confiscated *ex post facto* without a penny of compensation hundreds of millions invested in the liquor business. All this, too, was in labour-made property, not in law-made property, which greatly strengthens the precedent.

is to abolish even that State-organization which itself at present maintains.[1] It is too early for any forecast to be made concerning the outcome of this attempt; but whether it succeeds or not, the Russian Revolution has already performed an inestimable service to the world in proclaiming that the nature of freedom is not political but economic, and in refusing, as a State-organization, to use its power for the maintenance of an idle, rent-consuming class, living by the exploitation of labour at home or in spheres of influence abroad.

In order to abolish privilege it is not necessary, in a political democracy, to wait for the economic breakdown which its exactions inevitably bring about—that is to say, it is not necessary to wait until the number of wasteful idlers that production must support shall become so numerous and so wasteful that it can no longer meet their exactions. The ballot has been a pretty ineffectual weapon in the hands of the rank and file, but—so much must be said for republicanism—it could be made effective. First, however, the rank and file would

---

[1] The Constitution of one of the Soviet Republics—I think it is Georgia—begins something after this fashion: "It is the purpose of this Government to abolish government."

have to learn what it is that this weapon should be used against—it would have to become aware of the nature of real freedom, and to wish real freedom to prevail. The power of privilege under republicanism depends not only on its control of wealth, but much more upon its control of thought and opinion. That a campaign of education among the voters can seriously endanger the position of privilege was proved in England during the great land-values campaign of 1914, which was cut short by the war. But the task of education is not easy, because of the conditions I have just been discussing, which obscure the essential nature of privilege, and of the State. We have had in this country a great deal of outcry against privilege, and it has aroused considerable popular sympathy; but the zeal engendered thereby has not advanced the cause of freedom, because the outcry was directed against the capitalist and the exploiting power gained by his fortuitous advantage from privilege, but not against privilege itself. The nature of privilege was obscured. It is evidently necessary, then, if the ballot is ever to be successfully employed against privilege, to know what privilege means and to clear away all confusion about it, so that the voters may see what is at fault in our economic system, and what remedial steps are necessary.

The essential nature of freedom has been already shown. It comes out in the abolition of monopoly, primarily monopoly of natural resources, resulting in complete freedom of the individual to apply his productive labour where he will. It is freedom to produce, and its corollary, freedom to exchange—the *laissez-faire, laissez-passer* of the Physiocrats. How this freedom is to be obtained is not for me to say. I am not a propagandist, nor do I regard the question as at present so important as that of establishing a clear understanding of the nature of freedom. When enough people come to see that the root of all bondage, economic, political, social—even the bondage of superstition and taboo—is expropriation, reimpropriation will not be long in following; and it may be achieved by a method quite different from all those which theorists have thus far devised. When people know what they need, they are usually pretty resourceful about finding means to get it; and so long as they do not know what they need, all the means of securing it that can be suggested, however excellent, must remain ineffective from the lack of sufficient will to use them.

II

In the foregoing chapters I have spoken of the effect that freedom would have upon this or that phase of human relations. There is really no field of human activity that would not be profoundly affected by it. A system of free economic opportunity would exert upon the lives of human beings precisely as great an influence as that exerted by the present economic system: that is to say, their mode of life, their education, their quality of spirit, their cast of thought, would all be determined by their command of wealth, precisely as they now are. But where the present economic system operates to place the great mass of wealth at the command of a very small percentage of the population and thus to keep the majority in an involuntary and oppressive poverty unfavourably affecting body, mind and spirit in a thousand ways, a system of free opportunity would place in the hands of every human being all the wealth that his labour, freely employed, could produce, and at the same time it would relieve productive labour from the heavy burden of privilege. Thus that huge share of wealth which now goes to maintain the privileged classes in luxurious idleness, and that further huge share which supports vast bureaucracies and keeps up armies and navies to secure the foreign investments of the privileged classes, would be diverted to its proper use. The number of workers would be augmented by all those privilegees and placeholders who now live without producing;[1] but opportunity would be increased in infinitely greater proportion; therefore these newcomers would find no difficulty in supporting themselves. On the other hand, the immense reduction in luxury and waste thus brought about would very much shorten the hours of labour. The worker whose labour, in addition to maintaining himself and his dependents, is supporting two or three idlers and paying for a share of governmental waste besides, must necessarily spend many more hours at work than the worker whose exertions are required only for the support of himself and his natural dependents. But while the labour of each producer would decrease, production would be increased by the opening of new opportunities, by the increase in number of the producers, and by the enhanced power of consumption

---

[1] The political placeholder must not be confused with those workers in business, industry, or the arts who are not manual labourers, but perform valid services which are exchangeable for wealth and justify their being accounted productive workers.

made possible through their greater command of wealth. The redistribution which would follow upon the establishment of free opportunity, and the curtailment of waste, would satisfy a share of this new demand; but just as production and exchange, in a period of comparative prosperity at present, are stimulated by the increased consuming power of the public, so, when artificial restrictions on production had been removed, the increased power of consumption which would result would act as a permanent stimulus to production and exchange.

I will not speculate about the conditions arising during the period of adjustment to the new conditions of economic freedom. If bad, they would be but temporary, and though they are often magnified as arguments against freedom by those who either can not or do not wish to see beyond them, they have no proper place in this discussion, which is concerned only with the permanent effect of free opportunity on the lives, spirits and minds of human beings. It may be doubted that the intercalary hardships of the transition would be great; but if they were to be twice as great as the most timorous would forecast them, would they not be preferable to those attending the protraction of the present system to its inevitable break-up? That is the real question. Thomas Jefferson said that rather than the French Revolution should fail, he would see half Europe perish, and "though but an Adam and Eve were left in every country, and left free, it would be better than it is now."

Who can picture the profound alteration in the attitude of people toward life and their fellow-beings, if they were but emancipated from the fear of want which now besets all of humankind? Even the rich and the well-to-do are not exempt from this fear; for an economic security based on an unsound economic system is like those walks which are thrown along the thin crust of earth among the geysers of Yellowstone Park, where those who walk them are in danger that a misstep may plunge them through the thin crust to perish in the scalding heat beneath. While an economic system based upon the legalized robbery of one class by another remains in force, the abyss of involuntary poverty will always yawn for those who may lose their command of wealth through their own incapacity for management, or through circumstances beyond their control. It seems likely that an instinctive sense of this is at least partly responsible for the constant effort of people already well off to increase their fortunes. It is certainly responsible for a great deal of effort to get wealth by dishonest means—that is to say, by those forms of dishonesty which are without legal sanction. The fear of want produces avarice, chicanery, fraud, servility, envy, suspicion, distrust. It leads to unlegalized theft, to murder, to prostitution. It produces a class of people who, in a society which denies free opportunity and puts a premium on graft, live by their wits, and in so doing often display an energy and ability which would be useful to a society that offered it no opportunity save that for honest and useful employment. Moreover, this fear of want keeps the great majority of people constantly occupied with the means of existence, when they should properly be devoting a large share of their time to the fulfilment of its purpose, which is that enjoyment gained from developing one's spiritual capacities and pursuing spiritual interests. Those thus preoccupied can not employ with either imagination or profit what leisure they have. Rather, they will merely use their leisure to overcome their weariness of themselves. Their pleasures will be mere pastimes, of the kind that subvert thought and dull imagination. Thus little scope is left for the higher activities of the spirit, and the quality of life is impoverished.

The spiritual effects of the fear of want are naturally most clearly observable in countries where it is most widespread and deep-rooted. England offers a particularly good field for observation of these phenomena, for economic exploitation by a conquering class which has merged into a powerful owning aristocracy, is there advanced to the point of breakdown; therefore all the results of economic exploitation are present in overflowing measure. The most striking, perhaps, are the servility and snobbery which find sanction even in the Church catechism, in the passage admonishing candidates for confirmation to order themselves lowly and reverently unto all their betters—that is to say, those born to a higher place in the social order. The English novelists, from the days of Richardson and Fielding down to the present, have faithfully recorded the unlovely characteristics bred in a people by the ever-present necessity of keeping an eye to the main chance; by the knowledge that fortune may depend less on merit and ability than on a servile currying of favour with those powerful persons who, through the fortuitous circumstance of birth, are in control of economic opportunity. Richardson was himself demoralized by the social system to which the economic system had given rise. His acceptance of arrogance in the owning class and abjectness in the exploited, shows how acquiesence in injustice can corrupt even a man of genius. "Pamela" is a veritable study in servility; an unconscious and devastating exposition of the basic principle of English society. Fielding, on the other hand, was too critical to be corrupted by it, and his books are all the more valuable for the objectivity with which he presents the demoralization that a predatory economic system has produced. What an array of characters he parades before his readers—avaricious, envious, suspicious, self-seeking, arrogant, venal! Even the hero of his great novel, "Tom Jones," is not above prostituting himself to an elderly lady of wealth when he finds himself in danger of want and with no more honest means of getting a living, having been brought up as a gentleman, that is to say, an idler. This greatest of English novelists was well aware of the effect produced on the collective life of his nation by an arbitrary division of human kind into "High people and Low people," and he took occasion to comment upon it with a penetrating satire.

What Is To Be Done

Now the world being divided thus into people of fashion and people of no fashion, a fierce contention arose between them; nor would those of one party, to avoid suspicion, be seen publicly to speak to those of the other, tho' they often held a very good correspondence in private . . . but we who know them, must have daily found very high persons know us in one place and not in another, today and not tomorrow; . . . and perhaps if the gods, according to the opinions of some, made men only to laugh at them, there is no part of our behavior which answers the end of our creation better than this.

One might say that the profuseness of unamiable qualities with which Fielding endows so many of his characters, was due to a peculiar humour or pessimism in this writer, if one did not find those same qualities plentifully distributed among the characters of his successors. Dickens created a whole gallery of highly interesting and unadmirable folk, and one finds such faithful counterparts in Thackeray, for example, or in George Eliot, that they are to be explained not as the mere creation of any author's imagination, but as a product of the society in which he lived and observed.

There is material for an excellent study of the

relation of the economic and social system to the literary art, in the important rôle that money plays in English fiction. That intense preoccupation with the means of existence which is enforced by the fear of want, has profoundly affected the plots and characters of English novels. The number of plots which hinge on someone's attempt to get someone else's money, is astonishing. The number of men and women who either marry or attempt to marry for money, is legion; and no English novelist has the hardihood to settle his characters for life without providing them with a living, generally through inheritance or the generosity of some wealthy patron. It is significant that if they are going to make their own fortunes they usually strike out to make them in the new world, where there is some opportunity. The preoccupation with getting money, not through industry but through inheritance, cadging, or chicanery, is reduced to its lowest terms in the stories of W. W. Jacobs about life along the waterfront of London. These entertaining and racy stories, with monotonous regularity, present one theme, and that theme is the attempt of one character to do another —usually his closest associate—out of some trifling sum of money. It is interesting to note that one of the striking differences between English and American fiction is that where the former deals with money-getting the latter is likelier to deal with money-making. The one represents a society where opportunity is pretty thoroughly monopolized; the other a society in which it is as yet somewhat less so.

It is not the fear of want alone which demoralizes and corrupts. In a society where the greatest respect is paid to those who live in idleness through legalized theft; where men of genius may be treated like lackeys by those whose only claim to superiority is their command of wealth; where industry and ability yield smaller returns than flattery and servility; in such a society there is little to encourage honesty and independence of spirit. So long as honour is paid to those who live by other people's labour, in proportion to their power of commanding it, so long will praise of honesty, industry, and thrift savour of hypocrisy, and so long will the mass of people be under small temptation to cultivate these virtues; and so long, also, will the moralists who seek to inculcate them be open to the same suspicion of insincerity as are those bankers who stand to profit substantially by the thrift they preach among depositors. There is something grimly amusing in the complaints so frequently heard from those who live in ease, about the shiftlessness of the working classes and their dishonest workmanship; complaints which are well founded, perhaps, but do not take into account the slight incentive that is furnished by the knowledge that the profits of industry and honest workmanship will be diverted into other pockets than those of the workers. If labour takes every opportunity of giving as little as it can for as much as it can get, one must remember that it but follows the example set by the owning classes, an example that has yielded them rich returns both in wealth and in the esteem of their fellow-men. Under a free economic system no such demoralizing example would exist. The material rewards of honesty, industry, and thrift would accrue to those who practised these virtues; and since there would be no opportunity to gain esteem through the appropriation of other people's labour, those who wished to enjoy it would be forced to depend on more worthy means, such as ability, integrity, and uprightness in their dealings with other people.

In a free society, ignorance, vice and crime would tend to disappear. We should have no people in high places whose large-scale theft would make them fitter inmates for jails, and no people in jails for those petty thefts to which need is a perennial incentive. Jails, indeed, would be very little needed by such a society; for what with the abolition of the State, with its long list of law-made crimes, and the disappearance of those social conditions which are largely responsible for the few infractions of moral law which constitute real crime, there would be very few offenders to occupy them. I have already remarked that need is a constant incentive to theft; it is also the chief cause of ignorance; and ignorance and misery are fecund sources of vice, as well as of the physical and mental degeneracy which result in imbecility and idiocy. If need were removed, if every human being were assured from birth of physical well-being and ample opportunity to develop mentally to the full extent of his capacity, these distressing results of involuntary poverty would not long exist to menace the peace and health of communities and fill reformers and eugenists with alarm. The cities where human beings are crowded together under conditions subversive of health and decency would be gradually emptied of their surplus population. At present they are largely asylums for the expropriated, but when land was once more freely available they would resume their natural character as centres of industry and exchange. There would be no more centres of want, misery and vice, like centres of infection, to menace the health and well-being of society. Man, reclaimed by the land which is his natural home, would appear for what he really is, a child of the earth, rather than an industrial machine far removed from his rightful heritage of close, health-giving connexion with the soil from which his sustenance comes. Life, in short, having been placed on its natural basis, might be expected to proceed along natural lines of development. Mankind, assured of physical health, would progress steadily in health of mind and activity of spirit; and being freed from its pressing need to take thought of the morrow, it would have leisure to seek the kingdom of heaven—not that heaven which the church promises as a future reward for orthodox communicants, but the kingdom of heaven which "is within you," the happiness that comes from the harmonious development of the highest faculties of body, mind and spirit, and their use in the promotion of a beautiful individual and collective life. Superstition and intolerance would disappear with the ignorance that produces them. Thought would no longer be hampered either by fear or the consciousness of dependence on an order of things unfit to bear the light of reason; but every human being would be free to exercise that independence of mind that only the most courageous or the most securely placed may allow themselves at present. The long story of martyrdom for opinion would come to an end when freedom of opinion no longer threatened a vested interest in the perpetuation of injustice. Thus that "progressive humanization of man in society" which is civilization in the highest sense, would be in a way to be promoted as it has never been promoted in any society of which the world has knowledge.

III

Theoretically, it might still be possible for free economic opportunity and its benefits to exist for men only or for women only; but in order to exclude a whole sex from participation in them, it would be necessary to reduce its members to the status of chattels. Now, to reduce half of humanity to slavery is practically unthinkable; it would necessitate a reversion to an order of thought that has largely been outgrown; for all social injustice, in the last analysis, is founded in an ignorance and prejudice which cause even its victims to acquiesce in it. Indeed, without this acquiescence, social injustice may be called impossible. "After the primary necessities of food and raiment, freedom is the first and strongest want of human nature." Because of this instinct for freedom, the subjection of any class in society can be continued only so long as that class itself fails clearly to realize the injustice of its position; when it comes into a clear realization of this injustice it will demand and eventually obtain the removal of its disabilities. The subjection of women, such as it has been, lasted only so long as women themselves acquiesced in it.[1] When they developed a sense of injury, they began to demand the equality with men which is their right, and ignorance, prejudice and superstition are yielding before the de-

[1] This is not to be taken as a contradiction of what I have said in Chapter I concerning the argument that women wanted to be subjected. No class ever voluntarily accepts subjection; but when it has been subjected by one means or another, the ignorance that its subjection breeds may cause it to become passively acquiescent in the injustice of its position. It is worth noting that so long as the *idea* of slavery is tolerated, slaves may accept their position with a certain fatalism, much as the vanquished force in war accepts its defeat.

mand. There is no reason to suppose that women, having progressed thus far, would tolerate without a sharp struggle any reversion to the injustice from which they have escaped. Ignorance, prejudice, and superstition, moreover, are incompatible with the enlightenment which will be necessary in order to secure economic justice even for one-half of humanity; for that enlightenment postulates not only the desire to enjoy freedom oneself, but the desire that all people may enjoy it—that is, it postulates repudiation of the idea of dominance. Thus society not only could not endure half slave, half free; it would not wish so to endure.

Women are at present under certain disabilities which legal equality with men can hardly be expected to remove. Those disabilities are:

1. Economic: Women are the victims of unjust discriminations in industry and the professions in regard to training, opportunities, tenure of employment, and wages. They are also victimized by ill-considered "welfare" legislation sponsored by benevolent persons, and by male workers whose purpose is to rid themselves of unwelcome competition.[1]

[1] It is not to be understood that all male workers, individually or in union, take this attitude; but that it does exist among them I have already shown.

If legal equality of the sexes were established, women might be able, under the law, to force public industrial schools to give them equal opportunities for training; they might also be able to enforce a demand for equal pay with men for equal work. It is even conceivable that they might force employers to lay off workers, during periods of depression, on a proportional basis—men and women together, in proportion to the number of each sex employed. All this, however, would entail unremitting vigilance, and great effort in getting legal enactments; it would also entail a great deal of governmental machinery, with all the waste and ineffectiveness implied by the term; and it would leave the general labour-problem precisely where it is at present. As for the matter of opportunity, so long as industry is in the hands of private concerns, I see no way by which employers can be forced under an equal-rights law to employ women where they prefer to employ men. Nor is there any certainty that legal equality will save working women from having the race "safeguarded" at their expense. But if land were put freely in competition with industry for the employment of labour, all these disabilities would disappear. Women would enjoy the same freedom as men to get their living by their labour, and since there would be no such thing as a labour-surplus, their wage, like that of men, would be the full product of their labour, and not that share which employers or governmental boards thought fit to grant them. There would be no need for reformers or other benevolent persons to secure them fair hours and conditions of labour, or to get them excluded from hazardous employments; for there is no way to make a worker accept onerous conditions of labour from an employer if he have an ever-present alternative of going out and creating more agreeable conditions by working for himself. The worker whose independent position makes it possible to refuse to work an excessive number of hours or under unhealthful or dangerous or disagreeable conditions, will simply refuse, and there will be an end of it. Thus employers, instead of being prevented from exploiting women beyond a certain point, would be rendered incapable of exploiting anyone in any degree. Nor would male workers longer have any incentive to avail themselves of "protective" legislation in order to reduce the competition of women with men in the labour-market; for it is only where opportunity is artificially restricted that there are "not enough jobs to go around."

Certain direct consequences of the economic inferiority of women might be expected to disappear when that inferiority no longer existed. Foremost among these is the demoralizing temptation to get their living by their sex. Prostitution would disappear from a society which offered women ample opportunity to earn their living without doing violence to their selective sexual disposition. Marriage would no longer be degraded to the level of a means of livelihood, as it is today for a great many women; for economic security would no longer in any wise depend upon it. This being the case, the expectation now put upon women to undertake marriage as a profession would disappear, and marriage would come to be regarded in the light of a condition, freely and voluntarily assumed by both sexes, who would jointly and equally undertake its responsibilities. Under such circumstances, one might confidently expect a further modification of institutionalized marriage which would remove all those privileges and disabilities now legally enforced on either party by virtue of the contract. The idea that woman's place is the home—which implies that marriage, for her, necessarily involves acquiescence in a traditional sexual division of labour and a traditional mode of life—with all its disabling economic and psychological consequences, would disappear from a society in which she was able freely to choose her occupation according to her abilities. Thus, from the status of a class regarded as being divinely ordained to be the world's housekeepers, women would emerge into the status of human beings, free to consult their interests and inclinations in the ordering of their lives, without regard to traditional expectations which, being no longer enforced by economic or legal sanctions, would have no longer any power over them.

2. Psychological: Those prejudices and superstitions which now hamper women in their development and in the ordering of their lives, might be expected to disappear from a free society. In so far at they are the consequences of woman's subjection, they would yield before her emergence into the status of a human being, sharing equally with man in the freedom of opportunity that would result from the establishment of economic justice, and the increased cultural advantages that freedom of opportunity

would bring. In so far as they are the outgrowth of primitive ignorance and superstition, they would yield before the increased intelligence and enlightenment which might be expected to result from the abundance and leisure afforded to every human being by economic freedom. Thus those artificial differentiations between the sexes which have been built up by fear, by superstitions, and by masculine dominance, would tend to disappear. Women would no longer be regarded as extra-human beings endowed with superhuman powers for good or ill; they would no longer be regarded exclusively or chiefly as a function, being no longer forced to occupy that status; theories of their mental and spiritual inferiority based on the results of centuries of subjection would yield before a more humane and scientific attitude; and as freedom promoted individuation among women, it would become evident that the traditional notions concerning the feminine nature were drawn from qualities which, having been bred by their subjection, should have been regarded as characteristics not of a sex but of a class.

3. Social: The superstitious notion that woman's honour is a matter of sex would disappear with the masculine dominance from which it re-

What Is To Be Done 259

sulted. When women need no longer depend on marriage for their living or their social position, they will no longer be under any great compulsion to make their sexual relations conform to standards which have been adapted to suit the interests, desires and tastes of men. Being economically independent of men, they will be at liberty to consult their own interests, desires and tastes, in this as in other matters. They may desire to preserve those habits of virginity before marriage and chastity after it, which have been imposed upon them under masculine dominance; but they will be under no external compulsion to do so. When they have no longer a professional interest in conforming to the conventional moral code, their sexual relations will cease to be regarded as falling within the purview of morality at all; rather they will be, as those of men have been, a question of manners. For when a moral precept no longer has social or economic sanctions to enforce it, its observance ceases to be a matter of worldly interest or expediency, and becomes a matter of personal taste. Then, if it be not sound, it will be repudiated; if it be sound, the individual who allows himself to be guided by it will profit spiritually by doing so, because his obedience will respond to his own instinct for what is good, rather than to an external pressure.

The spiritual gain that will come through the release from bondage to superstition, discrimination and taboo, is incalculable. Freed from her slavery to catchwords, woman will be able to discover and appraise for herself the true spiritual values which catchwords usually obscure. Having no longer any need to preserve a fearful regard for what other people may think of her, she will be at liberty to regulate her conduct by what she wishes to think of herself; and hence she will be able to cast aside the hypocrisy, duplicity and dissimulation that must be bred in any class of people whose position in society depends not upon what they are but upon what they appear to be. Having attained to the full humanity which this emancipation implies, she will gain sufficient respect for her sex to tolerate no discriminations against it. Thus we may expect to see her sexual function of motherhood placed on a basis of self-respect, and the barbarous injustice of illegitimacy relegated to the limbo of forgotten abuses. Woman will for the first time undergo the profound and weighty experience of responsibility to herself, rather than to social institutions and arrangements

What Is To Be Done

which were made for her, and whose nature is not such as to command the deference of a free agent. Free from the tyranny of the expected, from the disabling consequences of surveillance and repression, women will for the first time be able to develop to their full stature as human beings, in accordance with the law of spiritual growth which has so long been thwarted and perverted by the usages of society.

I have given only a general idea of what economic freedom would do to promote human happiness. Its effect upon the lives and characters of men would be quite as emancipating as upon those of women; but this I have not space to consider in detail. In passing, however, I might remark that not the least of the benefits that men would gain by it would be relief from the worry and humiliation which the support of women so often involves at present. "I have taken mistreatment from that conductor," said a young musician recently, "that I never would have stood for if I were single. But I have a wife, and that makes us all cowards." A free people would outgrow on the one hand the sheepishness that fear of want begets, and on the other the arrogance bred by consciousness of power. Men would no longer need endure humiliation for the sake of keeping their jobs; and those over them would be estopped from arrogance by the knowledge that they were dealing with free men who were under no compulsion to tolerate it.

If it appear that I envisage utopian results from the institution of economic freedom, let me assume the possibility that those spiritual results which I foresee might not come about. If they did not come about, however, their failure to do so would imply a profound and inexplicable change for the worse in human nature; for if the world's history proves anything, it is that there is in mankind a natural disposition to aspire toward what is ennobling and beautiful, and that this disposition is favoured by economic security—especially where it is not associated with irresponsible power—and thwarted by involuntary poverty. Why is it that the middle classes are regarded as the "backbone" of society, if not because they have had enough command of wealth to enable the maintenance of health and a high standard of education, without that excess and power which too often breed idleness and arrogance? Leisure and abundance stimulate independence of spirit, thought, education, creative activity. Penury leads to demoralization, ignorance, dulness. This has been the world's experience in the past. "There is in man," says Goethe, "a creative disposition which comes into activity as soon as his existence is assured. *As soon as he has nothing to worry about or to fear,* this semi-divinity in him, working effectively in his spiritual peace and assurance, grasps materials into which to breathe its own spirit." Why should one assume that this spirit will pass over the material offered by life itself and the relations of human beings with one another? It has not done so in the past. Throughout mankind's long martyrdom of exploitation, through all the struggling and hatred engendered thereby, this semi-divinity in man has been leading him towards a more humane conception of life. The spiritual peace and assurance resulting from economic justice would set all human beings free not only to share in this conception but to realize it—to establish upon earth that ideal life of man which, in the words of George Sand, "is nothing but his normal life as he shall one day come to know it."

IV

The whole point of the foregoing, for present purposes, is this: It is impossible for a sex or a class to have economic freedom until everybody has it, and until economic freedom is attained for everybody, there can be no real freedom for anybody. Without economic freedom, efforts after political and social freedom are nugatory and illusive, except for what educational value they may have for those concerned with them. The women of the United States, having now got about all that is to be had out of these efforts—enough at any rate, to raise an uneasy suspicion that their ends are lamentably far from final—are in a peculiarly good position to discern the nature of real freedom, to see which way it lies, and to feel an ardent interest in what it can do for them. My purpose, then, is not deliberately to discourage their prosecution of any enfranchising measures that may lie in their way to promote, and still less to disparage the successes that they have already attained. It is rather to invite them thoughtfully to take stock of what they have really got by these successes, to consider whether it is all they want, and to settle with themselves whether their collective experience on the way up from the status of a subject sex does not point them to a higher ideal of freedom than any they have hitherto entertained.

In the past century, women have gained a great deal in the way of educational, social and political rights. They have gained a fair degree of economic independence. They are no longer obliged to "keep silence in the churches," as they still were at the beginning of the nineteenth century; indeed, certain sects have even admitted them to the ministry. The women who now enjoy this comparative freedom, and accept it more or less as a matter of course, are indebted to a long line of women who carried on the struggle—sometimes lonely and discouraging—against political, legal, social and industrial discrimination, and to the men, as well, who aided and encouraged them. Thanks to the efforts of these pioneers, the women of today have a new tradition to maintain, a nobler tradition than any of those which women were expected to observe in the past: the tradition of active demand for the establishment of freedom. They will be none the less under obligation to continue this demand when the freedom that shall remain to be secured is of a kind not envisaged by their predecessors. Rather, in the measure that they proceed beyond those ends that seemed ultimate to their predecessors, they will prove that these built well; for the best earnest of advancement is the attainment of an ever new and wider vision of progress.

The organized feminist movement in England and America has concerned itself pretty exclusively with securing political rights for women; that is to say, its conception of freedom has been based on the eighteenth century misconception of it as a matter of suffrage. Women have won the vote, and now they are proceeding to use their new political power to secure the removal of those legal discriminations which still remain in force against their sex. This is well enough; it is important that the State should be forced to renounce its pretension to discriminate against women in favour of men. But even if we assume that the establishment of legal equality between the sexes would result in complete social and economic equality, we are obliged to face the fact that under such a régime women would enjoy precisely that degree of freedom which men now enjoy—that is to say, very little. I have remarked that those who control men's and women's economic opportunity control men and women. The State represents the organized interest of those who control economic opportunity; and while the State continues to exist,

What Is To Be Done 267

it may be forced to renounce all legal discriminations against one sex in favour of the other without in any wise affecting its fundamental discrimination against the propertyless, dependent class—*which is made up of both men and women*—in favour of the owning and exploiting classes. Until this fundamental discrimination is challenged, the State may, without danger to itself, grant, in principle at least, the claims to political and legal equality of all classes under its power. The emancipation of negroes within the political State has not notably improved their condition; for they are still subject to an economic exploitation which is enhanced by race-prejudice and the humiliating tradition of slavery. The emancipation of women within the political State will leave them subject, like the negro, to an exploitation enhanced by surviving prejudices against them. The most that can be expected of the removal of discriminations subjecting one class to another within the exploiting State, is that it will free the subject class from dual control—control by the favoured class and by the monopolist of economic opportunity.

Even this degree of emancipation is worth a good deal; and therefore one is bound to regret that it has no guarantee of permanence more secure than legal enactment. Rights that depend on the sufferance of the State are of uncertain tenure; for they are in constant danger of abrogation either through the failure of the State to maintain them, through a gradual modification of the laws on which they depend, or through a change in the form of the State.[1] At the present moment the third of these dangers, which might have seemed remote ten years ago, may be held to be at least equally pressing with the other two. It is a misfortune of the woman's movement that it has succeeded in securing political rights for women at the very period when political rights are worth less than they have been at any time since the eighteenth century. Parliamentary government is breaking down in Europe, and the guarantees of individual rights which it supported are disappearing with it. Republicanism in this country has not yet broken down, but public confidence in it has never been so low, and it seems certainly on the way to dis-

[1] This is not to be taken as contradicting the earlier statement that women would not renounce without a struggle the rights they have gained. The world can not move toward freedom without carrying women along; they would not tolerate a dual movement, towards freedom for men and slavery for themselves. But when the general movement is away from freedom, as the movement of political government is at present, the rights of women are endangered along with those of men.

What Is To Be Done 269

aster. No system of government can hope long to survive the cynical disregard of both law and principle which government in America regularly exhibits. Under these circumstances, no legal guarantee of rights is worth the paper it is written on, and the women who rely upon such guarantees to protect them against prejudice and discrimination are leaning on a broken reed. They will do well to bear this in mind as they proceed with their demands for equality, and to remember that however great may be their immediate returns from the removal of their legal disabilities, they can hardly hope for security against prejudice and discrimination until their natural rights, not as women but as human beings, are finally established. This is to say that if they wish to be really free they must school themselves in "the magnificent tradition of economic freedom, the instinct to know that without economic freedom no other freedom is significant or lasting, and that if economic freedom be attained, no other freedom can be withheld."

CHAPTER VII

SIGNS OF PROMISE

SUPERFICIALLY it may seem that the present is an inappropriate time to suggest that either women or men go deliberately out of their way to undertake a process of self-education in the meaning of freedom. The dominant spirit among us is not only not hospitable to the idea of freedom; it is openly inimical to the idea. The United States is the richest and most powerful country in the world. It is in the midst of the most interesting experiment ever seen in the simplification of human life. It is undertaking to prove that human beings can live a generally satisfactory life without the exercise of the reflective intellect, without ideas, without ideals, and in a proper use of the word without emotions, so long as they may see the prospect of a moderate well-being, and so long as they are kept powerfully under the spell of a great number of mechanical devices for the enhancement of comfort, convenience and pleasure. This experiment is so universal and so preoccupying that while it is going on there would seem to be no chance to get any consideration for so unrelated a matter as freedon. Hence the only current notion of freedom is freedom to live and behave as the majority live and behave and to desire what the majority desire; and notions which diverge from this have not been under stronger suspicion and disapproval since the eighteenth century than they are in this country today. Not that any one, probably, fears any degree of liberty for himself, but every one has a nervous horror of too much liberty for others. Most people no doubt feel that they themselves would know exactly what to do with freedom and therefore might be safely trusted with any measure of it; it is the possible social effect of other people's liberty that they dread. No idea, probably, is more distrusted and feared among us at the present time than that of freedom for someone else.

The dominant spirit at present—the spirit which gives tone to our society—is diametrically opposed to the spirit of freedom. It is a spirit of coercion and intolerance. Politically this spirit finds expression in a pronounced reaction from the "progressivism" which had gained so much support before the war; in an enormous strengthening of "the cohesive power of public plunder," with a consequent reversion to the regimentation of strict party-government; in outrages committed by government, with popular approval—or at least indifference—upon the persons and property of people suspected of economic unorthodoxy; and in a cynical disregard by both government and populace of those guarantees of individual liberty which were wrested from government by more liberty-loving generations than our own. It is evident also in the development of extra-governmental organizations committed to a programme of violence actuated by religious bigotry, race-hatred, or inflamed chauvinism, such as the Hackenkreutzers and Fascists abroad—for the spirit of intolerance is not confined to the United States—and the Ku Klux Klan in this country; movements which, although they imply no menace to the exploiting classes themselves, do constitute a menace, at present imperfectly perceived, to the established organization through which those classes exercise exploitation, and an extremely threatening danger to the lives and liberties of millions among the governed.

Economically the spirit of coercion is in evidence in the struggles for advantage between capital and

Signs of Promise

labour, each trying to force the other to its own terms; in attempts by employers to break up defensive organization among their workers; and in such laws as the Criminal Syndicalism Acts, most of which give criminal character to membership in an organization professing radical economic doctrine. Socially it is reflected in such laws as the Eighteenth Amendment and the Volstead Act, and in puerile and evil-minded attempts at censorship of individual conduct, of public amusement, and of literature and art. In religion it is manifest in the activities of the Ku Klux Klan, in the current controversy between Fundamentalism and Modernism in the Protestant churches, and in the attempt sponsored by bigoted and influential church-organizations to stop by edict the progress of biological and anthropological science, because it threatens the tenure of established superstitions. It is likewise evident in the concern of those organizations with such social behaviour of individuals as must rationally be held indifferent, and their efforts to get their particular code of conduct enforced through sumptuary law.

The recrudescence of this spirit is the immediate result of war, which always brings it about. War embodies in its crudest form the doctrine of government by violence; and when war is dominant, therefore, the ideals of justice and liberty, which are directly opposed to it, become so unpopular that those who continue to profess them are liable to persecution by government and by their war-mad compatriots. Governments, which never grant their citizens more freedom of opinion and action than is absolutely necessary in order to get themselves tolerated, take advantage of this war-spirit to revoke, in practice if not in law, those guarantees of individual rights which it suits their purpose to dispense with. When the popular orgy of patriotic bloodthirst and intolerance is over, and the populace begins to get back to sanity, it finds government more securely fixed upon its back than ever, and prepared to ride it without that easy rein and that sparing of the spur which fear compels. Thus it is that the Governments of the Western world, since the war, have been carrying on their imperialist activities abroad and persecuting dissenters at home, with an excess of cynicism which would have been effectively reprehended by public opinion before the war.

The chief reason why this policy of force continues to command a large measure of popular support is because fear of bolshevism has taken the

Signs of Promise 275

place of that fear of the enemy which unifies public opinion behind Governments in war-time. Economic interests immediately consolidated against the influence of the Russian Revolution precisely as they did against that of the French Revolution, and in the same way. Governments have done all in their power to inculcate fear of this influence upon their peoples; and in this they command the assistance of practically the whole institutional organization of their respective countries. There is other and far better reason for this propaganda than the mere need of a new bogey with which to cow the timorous and keep the disaffected under control. The idea of freedom which bolshevist Russia has launched is a distinct menace to political government and its beneficiaries, the owning classes. If the expropriated and exploited masses in other countries once get it through their heads that their primary interest is not political but economic, the days of political government will be numbered. The propaganda against bolshevism is therefore inspired by two motives: the wish to frighten peoples into approving suppression of those suspected of political and economic heresy, and the wish to divert attention from the idea behind the Russian Revolution through the moral effect of real or supposititious misbehaviour by the Revolutionary Government. It is a curious twist of human psychology that makes supposed outrages committed by a foreign Government five thousand miles away appear to justify actual and equal outrages by one's own Government in one's own country; and a proletarian dictatorship five thousand miles away appear to justify a dictatorship of the exploiting classes at home. The Soviet Government's alleged mistreatment of political dissenters is easily made effective in ranging popular opinion in this country behind governmental persecution and deportation of communists and anarchists. Reports of Red terror in Russia reconcile public opinion—or at least that portion of it which is articulate—to the reign of a White terror here. It would appear that the desirability of dictatorship and terrorism is not in question, but their colour. Civilized persons, perhaps, would find little to chose between Red terror and White terror, or a Red dictatorship and a White; they would probably elect to dispense with terrorism and dictatorship altogether; but civilized persons have nothing to do with framing the policies of government, and almost nothing to do with the formation of majority-opinion.

Superficially, then, an invitation to contemplate freedom seems untimely. The cause of freedom is neither popular nor fashionable; therefore it may seem unduly optimistic to expect that there will soon be an interest in it deep enough or general enough to move many people to inquire seriously into its meaning or its desirability. Such a study would imply a critical reappraisal of institutions to which fear of change impels the majority to cling with a tenacity out of proportion to the benefits to be derived from their preservation. In this country this fear of change is especially strong because, as I have remarked before, the exactions of monopoly have not yet advanced to the point of choking industry. Moreover, opportunities to enjoy monopoly are not as extensively pre-empted here as they are elsewhere; and therefore the chances of the individual to share in the loot of industry are much better. This fact tends to keep a great many people loyal to an economic and political order which offers them a chance, however remote, to live by the earnings of other people, and to make them inhospitable to an idea of freedom which threatens that chance. There is another factor, too, which must be taken into account, as explaining the hostility of our proletariat towards an experiment in proletarian government which might be expected to gain their tolerance if not their sympathetic interest: that factor is the tendency of human beings to prefer an immediate temporary well-being to an ultimate permanent well-being conditioned on the acceptance of immediate hardship or uncertainty. *"Après nous le déluge"* is a sentiment by no means peculiar to dissolute and irresponsible monarchs. Humankind has always shown a perfect willingness to let posterity pay its bills and atone for its misdeeds. Labour at present is comparatively well off in this country; and it is significant that just those sections of it that are most advantageously situated are strongest in their opposition to the bolshevist experiment, namely: the unions in the American Federation of Labour. One can not unreservedly condemn their attitude; there is much to be said for it. In a society organized as ours is, the mere loss of a job is, as I have remarked elsewhere, terrible enough to keep one's thoughts from wandering on burning ground. The labourer stands to lose through any radical economic readjustment quite as much as the monopolist, that is, his all. If his all be sufficient to keep him from want, he will naturally regard with apprehension any proposal to take it away for the moment, even for the sake of his own possible future advantage. The poor man, especially if he have a family, is likely to feel that a present sufficiency is worth much more than a future surplus. It is only when people have literally nothing to lose but their chains that they can face without fear the prospect of revolutionary change. If the existing economic order remains in force, that time will come in this country as it came in pre-revolutionary France, and something over a century later in pre-revolutionary Russia; and when it does, there will be plenty of active interest in freedom, and of underground movements to bring it about by revolutionary methods. But at present the "dissidence of Dissent and the protestantism of the Protestant religion," the Anti-Saloon League, the one-hundred-per-centers, the Ku Klux Klan, and the Republican party, are in unapproachable ascendancy.

This does not greatly matter. Force and proscription are in the long run invariably ineffectual against an idea. The idea released by the American and French revolutions—the idea of the right of individual self-expression in politics—prevailed over the combined forces of European feudalism; and the idea released by the Russian Revolution will prevail over the combined forces of European and American imperialism. For ideas can be fought neither with armies nor with persecutions; nor can attention be for ever diverted from them. The only thing that has effective force against an idea is a better one. Whether or not the Soviet Government succeeds in getting beyond dictatorship to the establishment of economic justice in Russia is not really important. If it should fail, its failure will not halt the progress of the idea that human freedom is fundamentally a matter of economics. Not even that acceptance in principle and denial in practice which is the chief characteristic of Liberal policy, can permanently defeat it. Sooner or later it will penetrate into human consciousness; it will become part of that consciousness; and it will prevail. Whether or not it will prevail during this era of the world's history is another question, whose answer will depend upon the readiness of mankind to assimilate and be actuated by it. If it is not assimilated in time to prevent the ruin of European civili-

Signs of Promise

zation, then its ultimate victory will take place in a future era, when European civilization has followed the way of other civilizations to oblivion.

The process of assimilation is even now at work; with what effectiveness one may deduce from the strength and determination of the forces arrayed against it. It was no love for the Czar and the Russian nobility that caused the Allied Governments to spend millions of dollars in support of Kolchak, Denikin, and Wrangel, just as it was no love for Louis XVI and the French nobility that sent the Duke of Brunswick into France at the head of the Allies' army. It was fear of the idea which animates the Bolshevist Government. It was not because the Allied Governments hated Germany less but because they hated the Bolsheviki more that they failed to assent to the Soviet Government's proposal to surrender Petrograd and Moscow, establish a front in the Ural mountains, and continue the war against Germany. It was not their belief in self-determination, but their desire to interpose a buffer State between the embattled proletariat of Russia and the embattled imperialists of Western Europe, that caused them to erect Poland into an independent State. Nor has anything but the most pressing economic necessity moved any one of the Western Governments to treat with the cynical realists of Moscow, who have repeatedly embarrassed Allied politicians by their persistent abstinence from the hypocritical cant of the diplomat who has predatory designs to justify. Nor was it any sudden access of friendliness for Germany, or any noble superiority to sectional jealousies and nationalist ambitions, that moved these same Governments to sign the agreement of Locarno; it was, rather, a desire to make common cause against a Government whose avowed purpose is to destroy the privileged interests by and for which they themselves exist. Need anyone suppose that they would do all these things if they believed that the Russian idea could be localized? Not even the desire of their privilegees to exploit the natural wealth of Russia could have brought about a Locarno agreement. It was their sense of a common danger that overcame their mutual jealousies and distrust; the danger that the proletarians of their own countries may, as their miseries increase, be moved to emulate the proletarians of Russia, that a sense of class-solidarity may overcome traditional and national antipathies, and move them to unite for the purpose of casting off their chains.

Signs of Promise

There are tendencies in post-war Europe and America which must be disturbing to the politician who knows how to interpret them, if there be such a politician; tendencies far more significant of future developments than the mere existence of organized revolutionary minorities or the activities of single communists or anarchists, and much more difficult to cope with. Chief among these is a growing disrespect for government; the progress of a healthy cynicism concerning its nature and purpose, and a promising disregard of those sumptuary laws which do not meet with the convictions or desires of citizens. This tendency is by no means confined to any disaffected group or class. The citizen who is most patriotic, and most wholeheartedly with his Government in its attempts to coerce other people, may not scruple to evade its attempts to coerce himself. There is no articulate sentiment in this country, for example, against the income-tax law; yet there are few citizens who will not evade its incidence if possible, and feel themselves quite justified in doing so. Or again, who has not heard people comfortably provided with contraband liquor remark that they believe prohibition to be an excellent thing for the country in general? People may support the policies of a Government who entertain no illusions whatever about the nature of its personnel—or about the policies themselves for that matter—but who support them as a matter of self-interest or because they see nothing better to do. But all this does not augur especially well for the hold of government upon the loyalty or imagination of the governed. It is a truism that the Government which tries to enforce one law to which its citizens do not subscribe, thereby engenders disrespect for all law, and thus weakens its authority. Again, the citizen who supports his Government through self-interest or inertia may oppose it through self-interest or because his inertia has been overcome. If he does not support it through respect, its hold upon him is tenuous and uncertain.

As for the growing numbers of the disaffected, they show their loss of faith in so-called representative government, and their sense of helplessness, by a practice of non-co-operation which is none the less real because it is spontaneous and unorganized. The number of qualified voters who abstain from using the ballot grows with every election; and this is not surprising, since every voter of any intelligence knows precisely what interests control government, and precisely what measure of self-determination his apparent choice between rival candidates involves. Even the old faith in Liberalism, or the belief that the masses may get some voice in government through "putting good men in office," is not what it once was. Liberalism displayed its true colours during the war, and since the war it has not been able to fool a great many of the people even part of the time. It is worthy of note that every war-Government of 1914 was a Liberal Government except Russia's. Mr. Wilson was a Liberal if there ever was one; and Mr. Wilson's Administration led the American people into a costly war which was of practical moment to only an infinitesimal minority of our population, and used the opportunity created by war-hysteria to perpetrate the most high-handed outrages against dissenters from his war-policy. Mr. Wilson may have been sincerely insincere, as one clever critic put it; but whether he was so or not, he gave the American people a thorough, high-priced lesson in the essential hypocrisy of Liberalism. Mr. Wilson, and his fellow-Liberals of Europe, showed the world that the real interests of Liberalism and those of Toryism are identical, and that when those interests are endangered it is impossible to distinguish between Liberal and Tory behaviour.

It has, indeed, become abundantly clear since the war that a realignment of forces is inevitable; a realignment which shall represent not merely two factions differing slightly in regard to the non-essentials of government but one in the fundamental purpose of furthering economic exploitation; but a realignment which shall represent the cleavage which exists already, and will be widened as time goes on, between those who wish to perpetuate economic exploitation and those who wish it abolished. The remark which one frequently hears, that the two great parties in this country represent the same interests, means that they are both maintained by, and directly represent, the interest of monopoly which is engaged in exploiting industry. Their superficial differences, even, are notoriously insignificant, and fundamentally their interests and their source of power are identical. The logical cleavage, therefore, is between members of those two parties with all mere Liberals and reformers, on the one side, and advocates of economic justice on the other. It is really too late for compromise; too late for government to do everything for the exploited masses except get off their backs, as the German Imperial Government did so admirably before the war. Governments have become too corrupt and too ruthless, and the interests behind them too greedy, to perceive the wisdom of such a course. If the policy of coercion is in the ascendancy, if the executive arm of political government is everywhere usurping the function of the legislative arm, if parliamentarism and republicanism seem about to merge into dictatorship, it is because the ruling classes are much more aware of the coming struggle than are those classes whose interests will range them on the other side; and if many people now support government whose interests are against it, it is because they have not yet awakened to a realization of their true position. The increasing cynicism of the governed concerning the nature and purposes of government really marks an important advance toward the new alignment of forces. It is not a long step from the realization that government does not represent the general interest, to a discovery of the direction in which that interest lies.

Along with this cynicism go other signs of a changing attitude. There is a conspicuous falling off of faith in what might be called the unofficial adjuncts of government, namely: the press and the pulpit. The changing attitude towards organized religion was recognized and defined in the Pope's recent Encyclical Letter condemning the progress of laicism in all the countries of the Christian world, and the accompanying tendency to discuss Christianity as if it were merely one of the historical faiths, like Mohammedanism or Buddhism, instead of the only true, revealed religion. It is recognized also in the attempts to which I have alluded above, by certain Protestant sects in this country to secure laws forbidding the teaching of the theory of evolution. It is true that science and the printing-press have robbed a secularized church of its main source of influence over the minds of men, the one by discovering and proclaiming the natural laws behind those phenomena which ignorance attributed to benign or evil spirits; and the other by facilitating the general dissemination of knowledge. The Church can no longer effectively appeal to fear. For a church which very early became a class-organization, and one of the large-scale promoters and beneficiaries of economic exploitation, this is a serious thing. Its promises and its comminations are becoming alike ineffectual in face of mankind's growing concern with the spiritual effect of involuntary poverty and wretchedness upon the human spirit in this present world. The modern cynicism towards paternalism in government and industry finds its counterpart in cynicism concerning organized Christianity. In an age which questions the justice of mankind's arbitrary division into classes, such an Encyclical as that of Pope Leo XIII which enjoined masters to be lenient and the subject masses to be patient is already an anachronism; and the injunction put by the Church of England upon candidates for confirmation to order themselves lowly and reverently unto all their betters is more likely to arouse antagonism than to win compliance. The churches do not understand the new psychology with which they have to deal. They are offering dogmatic creeds to an age which is suspicious of all dogma; they are upholding traditional moral criteria in an age when the foundations of factitious morality are being generally scrutinized by the light of reason and knowledge; they are preaching salvationist doctrine in terms which no longer edify or recommend themselves to serious attention. All this is merely to say that organized religion, like political government, remains static in the midst of flux; and like political government it faces a spontaneous and widespread if entirely unorganized popular movement of non-coöperation.

As for that large majority of prosperous newspaper-concerns which are stigmatized in socialist literature as the "kept press," they have been so over-eager in the partisanship of their editorial writing and in the colouring of their news or its manufacture out of whole cloth, that there is discernible a decided change in the popular attitude towards them. The power of the printed word is still great out of all proportion to its weight; but editorial pronouncements, if they are read at all, are by no means swallowed as the undiluted milk of the word, as they were in the day when Horace Greeley used daily in the *Tribune* to dictate opinion to a large section of the American public. It is significant that since the advertising department has come to take precedence over the editorial department, there has been a decided falling-off in respect for journalism and a marked decrease in the number of honest and able people who take up journalistic work. This was to be expected. The modern newspaper is essentially an advertising medium, and its editorial writing and presentation of news must conform to its general

Signs of Promise

character. Under these circumstances men of intellectual ability and integrity are no longer attracted by such work, as they are no longer, for an analogous reason, attracted to governmental office or to the pulpit. The consequent deterioration in journalistic personnel contributes further to the newspaper's loss of prestige—again as in the case of the personnel of government and of the churches. As all those institutions lose the power to command respect and allegiance, they progressively lose power to attract able and honest minds to their service; and as they lose this power of attraction, their power to command respect progressively dwindles; and thus by alternate reactions they tend to disintegration. To return to the press, it is symptomatic of the loss of popular faith in its moral and intellectual character that people buy this newspaper or that so largely because of special features—local news, sporting news, this person's column or that person's cartoons. It is no exaggeration to say that the overwhelming majority of Americans look to their newspapers not for information but for entertainment or excitement; a fact which is amply attested by the amount of space devoted to special features, comic strips and cheap stories, and above all by the extraordinary success of a new tabloid type of newspaper devoted almost exclusively to pictures, accompanied by the most sensational kind of backstairs gossip. In the parlance of the street, the modern newspaper is "giving 'em what they want"; and while the preference is a sad reflection on public taste, its gratification is an equally sad reflection on the quality and standing of American journalism. The newspaper, in short, as I have said, no longer informs or guides opinion; it purveys amusement.

The same deterioration, with concomitant loss of prestige, that is proceeding in government, the church and the press, is evident in educational institutions. This is a natural and inevitable development, since education is so largely under political control. The powers which control government are in control of education; and those powers quite naturally will not tolerate any teaching which even implies a revaluation of the existing economic, political or social organization. This intolerance is effective even in institutions not under direct control by the State; for those institutions are largely dependent on wealthy benefactors, and wealth is almost entirely in control of people who have a direct interest in the preservation of the established order.

Under these circumstances, the primary purpose of education, which is to develop the mind and help it to independent progress along the paths of truth and reason, is rendered impossible of fulfilment; and our schools have pretty generally substituted for this purpose another and lower one which is calculated neither to embarrass nor offend the powers on which they depend. This is the vocational purpose. Thus they have ceased to be centres of culture, and become centres of training whose object is to turn out graduates who shall resemble one another as closely as possible in all things save in special vocational training. As Professor Jerome Davis recently expressed it, our colleges are turning out machine-made minds. The deterioration in the personnel of the teaching profession is consequently quite as marked as that in government, the churches and the press. Independence of spirit is not tolerated by school-directors and boards of regents. Teaching, moreover, being held in little respect by the State, to whose interests it is obviously inimical if prosecuted intelligently and seriously, is so poorly paid that people who can possibly do better elsewhere are naturally unwilling to become teachers. It is needless to dwell upon the demoralizing and vulgarizing effect of these circumstances on the schools themselves and those who attend them. It is too obvious and has been already too often discussed, to require consideration here. What I do wish to note is the fact that this educational system does not escape criticism and distrust; and that the most interesting and promising manifestation of this distrust is evident not among outsiders or alumni, but among undergraduates. Too much may not be expected of it, but the "youth-movement" which is afoot among students may not be disregarded; it is symptomatic of a critical attitude and a spirit of revolt which may not be wholly without effect.

These are negative signs of progress, if one will, but none the less impressive for that. They indicate a growing sense of discomfort in the environment provided by established institutions, and a loss of faith in those institutions as they deteriorate under the spread of their own corruption. On the positive side one may cite the growing power of economic organization, and its tendency to displace political organization. The appearance in the American Congress of a group known as the "farm-bloc" is an interesting instance of this tendency.

Signs of Promise

Here is a group of political representatives with whom an economic interest is frankly placed ahead of political affiliation. They are primarily neither Democrats nor Republicans, neither conservatives nor progressives; they are primarily representative of a producing group. As such, they stand for a departure from the theory of representative political government, which assumes that representation shall be not industrial but geographic. According to this theory, the representatives from each arbitrarily fixed geographical unit are supposed to represent the interests of all the citizens within that unit. This evidently leaves out of account not only the fact that economic interests are primarily industrial or occupational and only secondarily and fortuitously sectional, but also the fact that the economic interests within a given area may be mutually inimical. In practice, of course, political representatives have really represented the dominant economic interest within their allotted territory, the interest which has exercised the strongest political influence; but since in theory they must represent all interests, they have not been able to represent that dominant interest openly, but have had to resort to subterfuge and dishonesty. Even the members of the farm-bloc, were they representing districts where agriculture was not the dominant industry, would no doubt be less open in their espousal of its interest. None the less they have dared, in disregard of party-discipline, to form a bloc which stands squarely for the interest of a producing class; and in doing so they have taken a step towards the system of industrial representation which has of late made great strides in European countries, more especially in Russia and Germany. Although the group which has taken this step may be unimportant politically, save when a close division chances to throw the balance of power into its hands, the step it has taken is of the utmost importance; for if economic representation should proceed until it eventually superseded geographical representation, the change would not only involve the destruction of the bipartisan machine which controls government in this country; it would naturally bring about an open alignment of the producing interests against the interests of exploitation, and thus make clear the final and fundamental issue of which I have spoken—the question whether economic exploitation is to be perpetuated or abolished.

A good deal of non-political organization shows

the same trend. The growth of co-operation, for example, in production, marketing, and consumption, is evidence of an attempt to evade through group-action those exactions of government's beneficiaries against which the single individual is powerless to protect himself. The growth of offensive and defensive organization among capitalists on the one side and workers on the other, not only implies recognition of the primary importance of economic interests and the value of co-operation among groups whose economic interests are identical; it implies also an acknowledgment that neither capital nor labour receives from government what it will accept as adequate protection of its interests —as, of course, neither can, since the interest that government exists to protect—the interest of monoply—is directly inimical to both. Moreover, as this organization becomes international in scope it constitutes a negation of the political differences which bolster up rival national organizations. That it has not yet become strong enough to prevent nationalistic wars, is true; but this is because the fact that war is a clash, not of rival producing interests, but of rival exploiting interests has not yet become sufficiently clear to overcome a specious patriotism and the traditional distrust and prejudice which governments have assiduously inculcated upon the governed. The producing classes are really behind the exploiting classes in discovering that their interests are pretty much the same, whatever their various nationalities may be. Governments have always co-operated when any rebellious move by the governed in any country threatened the established economic and political order; as they co-operated in the Holy Alliance against France, or in a similar alliance against Russia, and as they are now co-operating in the League of Nations against the exploited classes in all countries. When the exploited classes understand their own position as clearly as the exploiting classes have understood theirs, organization for defense and offense will no longer be national and vertical but horizontal and international. The real issue will be drawn at last. Hence the tendency of capital and labour toward international organization along the lines of economic interest is an extremely hopeful sign that the producing classes are beginning to realize that their major interests are not political but economic, and that the quarrels of Governments are injurious to those interests; that they are beginning to outgrow the narrow nationalism which has facilitated their exploitation in the past, and made it possible to pit them against one another in the quarrels of rival exploiting classes.

II

All these signs of disaffection under the old order of things and the gropings towards a new, do not imply, of course, any growth of the spirit of freedom, or any new consciousness of its nature. They do indicate, however, the progress of a temper which, when it shall have become more pervasive and more deeply rooted, will be hospitable to the doctrine of freedom. Discontent with the established order must necessarily precede any serious move toward its displacement by a new order; and discontent, while it is by no means dominant at present, is widespread enough to cause Governments a good deal of anxiety. The very tightening of the grip of government which is evident in the present tendency to suppress legislative bodies, and in ruthless persecution of economic dissenters, is, as I have already remarked, a sure indication of the extent and strength of the dissenting forces. When those people who now endure the harassment of governmental waste and industrial exploitation, shall perceive that relief is to be gained not through futile political reforms aimed at amelioration of their lot, but through a radical readjustment of the whole economic system—when, in other words, they realize "what is to be done"—then and not before, will come the real test of the tenacity of the old order and the strength of the forces moving towards the new. On its side the old order will have governmental organization and armed forces, and the enormous influence of the superstitious tendency to regard as right that which is established, supporting the interest of a compact, wealthy, and highly organized exploiting class. The new order will have on its side the newly realized need of the majority without whose acquiescence a highly organized minority can not long maintain itself in power. The issue will depend, obviously, not only on the intelligence, ability and determination of the majority's leaders, but upon their clear understanding of the issue involved. If they compromise, as the leaders of the French Revolution compromised, the cause of justice will be lost, and the most that will be gained will be a shifting of privilege. The Western world is faced at present with the alternative of establishing an enduring civilization on the sure foundation of economic justice, or of sinking back into barbarism through a long series of civil and international struggles for possession of the power to exploit. If it follow the latter course, its civilization will go the way of the civilization of Egypt, Greece, and Rome; and its vitality, like theirs, will so decrease under the dual drain of exploitation and war that it will eventually fall, as they fell, an easy prey to some strong external force.

The task before those who wish to avert this fate, whose passionate desire is to bring about an enduring civilization based on the solid foundation of economic justice, is the task of educating themselves in the nature of freedom, of learning to face freedom without fear, and of communicating to others their understanding and their courage. The women of today, especially in this country, are in a peculiarly good position to undertake this task They enjoy unprecedented advantages in the way of social and intellectual autonomy, and of educational opportunity. They have emerged successful from a long struggle for political equality with men, and they are still engaged in an organized effort to secure legal equality. Thus they have their hand in, as it were, with the work of removing the artificial disabilities which organized society imposes on a subject class in order to keep it subject; and this work should have engendered in those who have been active in it a healthy resentment of social injustice and a sense of the value of freedom to the human spirit. They will still have, moreover, even after legal equality is won, a considerable number of discriminations to combat, which should operate against the temptation to regard their fight as won, and to relax the vigilance which is always necessary to preserve individual rights against encroachment by organized society. The organizations through which they have worked remain intact; it is for them to determine whether those organizations shall continue as mere agencies for political lobbying or whether they will carry on the demand for freedom to its logical end.

The fact that women are in a good position to inquire into the nature of freedom offers, of course, no earnest that they will do so. In spite of the reasonableness of such a course, they may content themselves with trying to effect the ultimate equality of the sexes through political measures which in their nature can never effect it—provided, that is, that events do not move too fast for even a serious trial of such inept methods. A good deal of mirth has already been aroused in certain quarters by trivial and futile reform-measures which women politicians have sponsored. If this sort of thing shall prove to be the sum-total of women's contribution to social problems, it will merely prove that they are quite as incapable of an intelligent understanding of those problems as men have hitherto shown themselves to be. If women are now in a good position to school themselves in the tradition of economic freedom, the men of Europe and America have been in an equally good position to do so since the political revolutions of the eighteenth century, and as yet they have given no very encouraging signs of progress. However much one may hope that women will make a better showing, it would be unfair to expect it of them; for they are but now emerging from the mental and spiritual condition induced by centuries of subjection. If, therefore, they fail to grasp their opportunity to contribute to the process of education which must precede the establishment of economic justice; if they are content to fix their minds upon this or that special aspect of social freedom or of political freedom, instead of looking steadily towards economic freedom—economic freedom for men and women alike—the judicious critic may lament their failure or disparage their tactics, but he can hardly attribute either to any stupidity or incapacity peculiar to their sex, since it is through the same failure and the same tactics that men have brought civilization to the critical state in which it is at present.

The great point, however, is that if they fail they are sure to pay for their failure a higher price than men will pay. As they have more to gain from freedom than men, so they have more to lose than men if the Western world shall fail to establish its civilization on the firm basis of economic justice. In the relapse into barbarism which must attend the ultimate breakdown of economic and social life under the monopolistic system, physical force will be even more strongly ascendant than it is at present; and when physical force dominates, the ideals of justice and liberty are, as I have already remarked, without effective influence—the only right is might. The well-being of women depends in very great measure on the prevalence of those ideals; for when force is dominant, woman's physical disadvantage as the child-bearing sex places her in a

Signs of Promise

position to be more readily subjected and exploited than man. Because of this disadvantage she was the first victim of exploitation; because of it, she will be the last to escape; and because of it she will be the greater sufferer from exploitation so long as exploitation shall be the basis of the economic and social order. There is potential tragedy in the fact that the Western world has become civilized enough to perceive the injustice involved in women's subjection only when the economic order which determines its social life has become so corrupt that it threatens the destruction of civilization, with all such gains in humanity as civilization has yielded. Women have equality almost within their grasp; they may lose it if this civilization shall follow the path of its predecessors to ruin and oblivion. There is one way to avert this tragedy, and one only—the way of economic justice. If the women who have been active in the struggle to emancipate their sex shall enlarge their conception of freedom, and with it the scope of their demand, they can help mightily to preserve civilization through the establishment of justice. If they could win their sex away from the exploded formulas of the eighteenth century and bring them to understand that political and social freedom without economic freedom are utterly illusory, that true freedom proceeds from economic justice, and that justice and freedom offer the only hope for the salvaging of this civilization, they would have won half of humanity, and that would be a contribution of no small value. One thing is certain: the question of freedom for women can not proceed much farther as an independent issue. It has reached the point where it must necessarily merge in the greater question of human freedom. Upon the fate of the greater cause, that of the lesser will depend. It is for feminists to choose whether they will merge the feminist in the humanist, or whether they will play at political and social make-believe while the issue is being decided, and either suffer in the event the consequences of a failure which they shall have made no effort to avert, or enjoy the benefits of a success which they shall have done nothing to attain.

American Women: Images and Realities
An Arno Press Collection

[Adams, Charles F., editor]. **Correspondence between John Adams and Mercy Warren Relating to Her "History of the American Revolution," July-August, 1807.** With a new appendix of specimen pages from the **"History."** 1878.

[Arling], Emanie Sachs. **"The Terrible Siren": Victoria Woodhull, (1838-1927).** 1928.

Beard, Mary Ritter. **Woman's Work in Municipalities.** 1915.

Blanc, Madame [Marie Therese de Solms]. **The Condition of Woman in the United States.** 1895.

Bradford, Gamaliel. **Wives.** 1925.

Branagan, Thomas. **The Excellency of the Female Character Vindicated.** 1808.

Breckinridge, Sophonisba P. **Women in the Twentieth Century.** 1933.

Campbell, Helen. **Women Wage-Earners.** 1893.

Coolidge, Mary Roberts. **Why Women Are So.** 1912.

Dall, Caroline H. **The College, the Market, and the Court.** 1867.

[D'Arusmont], Frances-Wright. **Life, Letters and Lectures: 1834, 1844.** 1972.

Davis, Almond H. **The Female Preacher, or Memoir of Salome Lincoln.** 1843.

Ellington, George. **The Women of New York.** 1869.

Farnham, Eliza W[oodson]. **Life in Prairie Land.** 1846.

Gage, Matilda Joslyn. **Woman, Church and State.** [1900].

Gilman, Charlotte Perkins. **The Living of Charlotte Perkins Gilman.** 1935.

Groves, Ernest R. **The American Woman.** 1944.

Hale, [Sarah J.] **Manners; or, Happy Homes and Good Society All the Year Round.** 1868.

Higginson, Thomas Wentworth. **Women and the Alphabet.** 1900.

Howe, Julia Ward, editor. **Sex and Education.** 1874.

La Follette, Suzanne. **Concerning Women.** 1926.

Leslie, Eliza. **Miss Leslie's Behaviour Book: A Guide and Manual for Ladies.** 1859.

Livermore, Mary A. **My Story of the War.** 1889.

Logan, Mrs. John A. (Mary S.) **The Part Taken By Women in American History.** 1912.

McGuire, Judith W. (A Lady of Virginia). **Diary of a Southern Refugee, During the War.** 1867.

Mann, Herman. **The Female Review: Life of Deborah Sampson.** 1866.

Meyer, Annie Nathan, editor. **Woman's Work in America.** 1891.

Myerson, Abraham. **The Nervous Housewife.** 1927.

Parsons, Elsie Clews. **The Old-Fashioned Woman.** 1913.

Porter, Sarah Harvey. **The Life and Times of Anne Royall.** 1909.

Pruette, Lorine. **Women and Leisure: A Study of Social Waste.** 1924.

Salmon, Lucy Maynard. **Domestic Service.** 1897.

Sanger, William W. **The History of Prostitution.** 1859.

Smith, Julia E. **Abby Smith and Her Cows.** 1877.

Spencer, Anna Garlin. **Woman's Share in Social Culture.** 1913.

Sprague, William Forrest. **Women and the West.** 1940.

Stanton, Elizabeth Cady. **The Woman's Bible** Parts I and II. 1895/1898.

Stewart, Mrs. Eliza Daniel. **Memories of the Crusade.** 1889.

Todd, John. **Woman's Rights.** 1867. [Dodge, Mary A.] (Gail Hamilton, pseud.) **Woman's Wrongs.** 1868.

Van Rensselaer, Mrs. John King. **The Goede Vrouw of Mana-ha-ta.** 1898.

Velazquez, Loreta Janeta. **The Woman in Battle.** 1876.

Vietor, Agnes C., editor. **A Woman's Quest: The Life of Marie E. Zakrzewska, M.D.** 1924.

Woodbury, Helen L. Sumner. **Equal Suffrage.** 1909.

Young, Ann Eliza. **Wife No. 19.** 1875.

301.412L165c
Concerning women

1144 00140946 4